Learning to Apply

Learning to Apply

Book Five

Quince Duncan

West Institute and School of Education

Text revision Cynthia Delgado
West College and Institute of Education
Illustrations Mariela Pérez and Quince Duncan
Special thanks to Kimberly Gutiérrez, Carolina Martínez, Federico Araya,
Ileana, Magaly and Beatriz Villalobos and West College High School professors and students.

Library of Congress Control Number: 2013901733
ISBN: Softcover   978-1-4633-5051-2
                 Ebook   978-1-4633-5050-5

This book was printed in the United States of America.

To order additional copies of this book, please contact:
Palibrio
1663 Liberty Drive
Suite 200
Bloomington, IN 47403
Toll Free from the U.S.A 877.407.5847
Toll Free from Mexico 01.800.288.2243
Toll Free from Spain 900.866.949
From other International locations +1.812.671.9757
Fax: 01.812.355.1576
orders@palibrio.com
436809

TABLE OF CONTENTS

A NOTE OF RECOMMENDATION

When reading this Manual, use your dictionary.

Almost all difficulties with studies are a direct result of the reader not having a full comprehension of the words he reads.

Furthermore, one of the objectives of this Manual is to widen the vocabulary of our students.

Readers should never ignore or bypass a word that they do not fully understand.

FIRST PART:
PREPARING FIELDWORKS

INTRODUCTION TO BOOK FIVE

Book Five of the Learning to Apply Series, is a consolidated version of two former manuals, titled Fieldworks (Duncan, 2010) and Applying Research (Duncan, 2010), used in 10th and 11th grades at West College High School. This reform, at the suggestion of Director Cynthia Delgado, is consistent with the fact that the undergraduate paper that West's students prepare is developed precisely over these two academic years as a single project.

During level ten-eleven, students consolidate their capacity for self-education — learning how to learn, learning how to comprehend the subjects studied, and learning how to apply the knowledge acquired when faced with today's challenging and changing reality, thereby achieving the final aim of the Series. Students will design and develop an undergraduate report, ("tesina" in Spanish) which is the final research-report that they are expected to present as part of their graduation process. The tesina is basically an individual study that each student carries out to demonstrate his capacity to formulate a problem, confront it with a basic theoretical framework, using proper methodology and adequate techniques required to close this stage of his academic experience. The course is divided in two parts: Fieldworks, designed to recap formerly acquired knowledge, to set up a professionally oriented research plan and to complete preliminary investigation. The second part, Applying Research, guides students to the completion of their investigation and to the delivery of a competent report.

What to Expect

West College High School students, to graduate from 11th grade, have to present their undergraduate report of a field research (tesina). In 10th grade, you must present your project and get it approved by the advisor and Integrated Projects Coordinator, and start working on your project throughout the year.

It has been highlighted during this Learning to Apply Series that West High School has adopted a holistic pedagogic strategy called SIPEIN that emphasizes the capacity of its students to do research. The system gears the student toward self-teaching. "The aim is that each student learns how to learn, learns how to comprehend whatever he studies, learns how to apply his knowledge when faced with today's challenging and changing reality" and learns how to be a person, a successful person.

These aims include developing an investigative attitude, to promote the student´s ability to formulate a problem; setup his or her own objectives, propose a hypothesis based on a research problem, choose an adequate method and its corresponding techniques; collect information in an orderly way to support the hypothesis or to accomplish objectives, and finally, to present their reports attractively and according to research standards—such is the profile of a student graduating out of the system.

Tutoring plays a very important role in this process. Your advisor is there to give a lending hand. His mayor responsibility is not to give you a grade, but to assist you in your task. But, success depends on your own efforts.

Throughout this course, you will be given an overview of the basic characteristics of a field research. You will be prepared to set up your undergraduate project. This year, you will do the planning and advance in the bibliographic research. At the end of the course, you will be required to give a partial report on your subject. Next year, according to school calendar, you will do your field works, prepare and defend your tesina publicly.

So, hear you go, on your way to the final adventure at West.

THEME 1 WEST COLLEGE PEDAGOGIC FOCUS.

> *ACTIVITY:*
> *Using the dictionary, look up the underlined words and clarify each of them, as well as any other word that you are not acquainted with. Make sure you have a thorough understanding of each word. Almost all difficulties with studies are a direct result of the reader not having a full comprehension of the words he reads. Remember that one very important objective of this Manual is to widen your vocabulary. Never ignore or bypass a word that you do not fully understand*

The learning theory underlying this manual of applied research in the field of education is a <u>holistic</u> vision and in this regard it is framed in the <u>systemic</u> educational philosophy exposed and practiced under different names in various institutions. It is a systemic applied <u>pedagogy</u>; stemming from a <u>perspective</u> of <u>totality</u>. Research is just one of the resources used in the realization of this vision.

The idea of this first theme is that you become aware of the School's perspective. There are five basic <u>postulates</u> supporting <u>SIPEIN</u>. The first <u>premise</u> is that the approximation to an object of study from a holistic perspective facilitates better comprehension. That is to say, when studying reality one should take a look at the forest, not limiting one's perspective to the individual trees. In other words, it is necessary to take into account the <u>context</u>.

From this viewpoint you are expected to see and understand the natural and social phenomena from a global perspective. As correctly stated by Maria Candida de Moraes, "everything that exists, coexists" (t.m.). This is the holistic view, implying that there is "interdependence and interaction between living organisms and the world of nature and is so with all beings" (Candida de Moraes. 1999: 73).

Another related opinion comes from Hurtado de Barrera (2000: 19) This Author rightly underlined human inability to exhaust the understanding of the reality with a single approach. Description of any <u>phenomenon</u> will always be more satisfactory and complete and <u>coherent</u> with the <u>whole</u>, if such a description stems out of the inputs from different areas, philosophies, methods and disciplines.

It is therefore necessary that you, as a researcher, develop such an overview of the research process that will enable you to have a better understanding of whatever theme you might choose to study, in present time (<u>diachronic</u> perspective) or in its historical context and <u>dynamic</u> (<u>synchronous</u> perspective). Accordingly, you must be aware of the fact that, for this holistic vision, the reality is dynamic and not <u>static</u>.

The second premise held by SIPEIN is that the whole is more than a simple sum of its parts, but also, that the whole cannot exist independently from its parts. The above brings up two fundamental ideas. In the first place the understanding that the "realities" that you will be investigating are made up by a series of items (things) that interact with each other to produce new realities that are more than the sum of these elements. Therefore, while keeping an eye on the totality, the researcher cannot ignore the parts, because ultimately, the whole would not be possible without these parts.

A good example in the physical world is water. Water is composed of oxygen and hydrogen. Breathing high concentrations of this gas is detrimental to health. Symptoms include headaches, dizziness, unconsciousness, nausea, vomiting and depression of all the senses. Under extreme circumstances the results might even be death. Yet, combined with oxygen, the outcome is water, an element indispensable for life. The whole, as we can see, is more than the sum of its parts, but water cannot exist without its parts.

The third premise is that there is continuous <u>alternation</u> and <u>interrelation</u> between the different phases of the research process. In effect, the phases of the research are not sequential, but simultaneous. During the exploratory phase, you may encounter analytical factors and while working on description prediction may occur. The apparent <u>linearity</u> when studying the research process is only for practical purposes, so that things can be done orderly but in the process of thinking conclusions may surge simultaneously.

Precisely, alternation and <u>concurrency </u>can lead to the modification of the original approach. A hypothesis requires confirmation, but in the process of experimentation you may discover a new theory (explanation) or could even come to the conclusion that your original hypothesis is incorrect. This is OK. If facts prove differently there are no qualms; just explain and change.

The fourth premise <u>postulates</u> that any change involves an exchange. The very intervention of the researcher alters the factors. Even a simple sampling involves, at least, a small modification. A limited survey could make people become aware of their reality and lead them to act differently. But also this principle alludes to the fact that the investigator could become involved in the process in a conscious way, which is only valid in the holistic approach. In fact, holism finds that the structures studied are but manifestations of underlying processes, to the point that the events are studied from an overall dynamic, according to their interrelationships (Hurtado de Barrera, 2000: 28).

The fifth premise postulates that we live in a changing reality and therefore knowledge is in the process of continuous construction. As worded by Maria Candida de Moraes, knowledge is something that is always in process of construction, transformed by the action of the individual in the world, the experience of the subject on the subject, its transformation into an active subject in a process of permanent construction. (Moraes: 1999: 11). From the above it can be deduced that the knowledge about a phenomenon or event, is never totally exact. Scientific knowledge is only a temporary but functional explanation of a set of facts, but it is always open to be replaced by new visions that can provide partial or radical changes.

The above principles require that the researcher cultivate a "panoramic view" allowing for a proper understanding of the phenomenon in present time and in its historical context. From the diachronic point of view, it imposes the enrichment of the research with earlier visions and paradigms. The reiteration of the following idea seems imperative: reality is complex and cannot be exhausted with a single perspective; we must enhance our understanding of it with an interdisciplinary approach, open to the ideas of diversity and change.

ACTIVITY:

Define the following terms using your own words:

Perspective
Holism
Process
To enhance
Systemic
Linear
Phenomenon
Postulate
Premise
Paradigm

THEME 2 SCIENTIFIC RESEARCH: THE SUPPORTING THEORY

It is always a good idea to remember that the word research is interchangeable with investigation. Investigation is a word taken from Latin, "in vestigium" meaning to follow a trail. In a wider definition, we can say that research is a working process in which a person (or team) starting with an idea, a project, a problem and using different instruments to achieve his goal—satisfy the drive for knowledge for himself, a group or a community (Duncan, et.al (1986, p. 15).

This "working process" is rigorous, reflexive, systematic, controlled and quizzical and the correct application of scientific methods used, lead to the discovery of new data, unexpected relations and scientific laws in the diverse areas of Human knowledge. Hurtado de Barrera (2002, pp. 41-42) sustains that this process is an organized continuum, evolving, seeking new knowledge on the bases of what is already known. This knowledge constitutes the backbone of technological advancement.

In our world, research is becoming more and more important. To compete with any probability of success, students as well as professionals have to develop investigative attitudes and capacity. "Bench" educational strategy, in accordance to which students learn passively what is being dished out to them by professors and recite or write the information received when tested, has long past its day. Much of the information handed down to the students in this outdated system, is not even understood—in fact, students do not have to understand the subject matter. All they are required to do is to "talk back" when asked to.

Howard Gardner (1991), has pointed out to the fact that some traditional educational approaches, sums up to an outrageous waste of time and effort. Elsewhere, we have argued that traditional education is an organized form of idleness designed to procure certificates for everyone.

Today, in our contemporary world, where cultures intermix and economies are closely tied together, it is the capacity to identify a problem, hypothesize about it, and using an adequate method to solve it, that is highly valued in our societies.

When growing up, I remember consulting a book that proposed a list of one hundred books and works of art that a well-educated person should master. It was a very simple recipe. Any one in command of those masterpieces could consider himself a well-educated and civilized citizen of the world. Today I don't think anyone would dare elaborate such a list. The world is changing in a pace that induces vertigo.

This has affected professions and professionals. There is only one way to keep up with the tremendous amount of changes going on in every field, and that is to develop a self-educational capacity, by means of a good training into the techniques of learning how to learn, learning how to comprehend the subjects studied, and learning how to apply the knowledge acquired when faced with today's challenging and changing reality.

Illustration 1. Working as a team.

ACTIVITY:
   Give examples of how a person:

> ✓ Learn to learn.
> ✓ Learn to comprehend what he is learning.
> ✓ Learn how to apply his knowledge.

Paradigms

Scientists claim that the scientific method is only one. But not all scientists approach scientific research from an identical standpoint. These different viewpoints are termed paradigms and to a certain extent they divide the scientific community. A paradigm is a model, a way to look at things. It is a set of theoretical considerations to which a group of scientist ascribes. It is the way in which the scientific researcher views the world. Every researcher, whether or not he is aware of this fact, follows a paradigm with more or less consistency.

Four major paradigms have been used over the last hundred years or so. They are called positivism, structuralism, pragmatism and — of later data, holism.

Positivism

Positivist scientists consider that the only true knowledge is that based on actual experience. This has been a very ancient idea in Western culture, but was developed by a 19th century philosopher whose name was Auguste Comte. He was followed by many others.

From the point of view of positivist researchers, reality is stable, and for that reason verifiable. There is an effort on their part to reduce reality to figures. The idea is to give universal validity to their discoveries. In the ultimate analysis, positivist researchers attempt to "provide evidence" for a supposition that they have made before hand — a hypothesis. Knowledge acquired in this fashion is considered by these researchers as superior to all other forms of perception of reality.

Structuralism

In the 20th Century, new trends appeared and found a place in the scientific community. One of these is called structuralism. Structuralist researchers attempt to analyze systems in their complexity. In the late 19th Century and early 20th Century Ferdinand de Saussure propose structuralism and applied it in the field of linguistics. But by the 50s, other intellectuals had appropriated this viewpoint and started applying it to other fields of study. Today, many disciplines use this approach to reality. Structuralist researchers consider that the structure of a system defines the position and function of each of its elements. For that reason, their main thrust is to discover "structural laws".

The important thing is not change but how the system does persist over time. To research is to analyze, to find and to explain the "significance" of the diverse elements of the whole.

Structuralist researchers are deductive scientists and for that reason do not generalize their findings. The findings are valid for the group studied, and although it might suggest possible explanation for similar phenomena elsewhere, it does not have universal validity. In this sense, the viewpoint of structuralism is entirely opposite to positivism.

Pragmatism

According to the pragmatic viewpoint, research is only justified if it produces something useful. That was the viewpoint adopted and promoted by Kart Lewin (1948). Research is done to solve a concrete problem, to introduce changes into a certain reality.

The first step is to explore the problem. Second, the researcher moves on to do an analytical study and third he is expected to propose a solution to the problem. Finally, he evaluates the procedures and steps taken and then adopts corrective measures. This method has been followed by many social scientists, especially in social psychology, education, political activism and administration.

Holism

Holism also appeared in the first half of the 20th Century. This viewpoint was proposed by Jan C Smuts (1926), a South African. The idea became well positioned during the 50s and 60s, when many Western intellectuals adopted and applied holistic views in doing research. "Holism" comes from the Greek word "holos" meaning the totality.

According to holistic researchers, the system or organism is more than the simple sum of its parts. Also, reality is so complex that it has to be analyzed from multiple perspectives. According to María Cándida Moraes, "everything that exists, co-exists" (1999, p. 73).

This viewpoint rejects the narrow notion that reality can be understood from a single paradigm. For that reason, multiple and inter-disciplinary research is basic to all studies. Things must be understood as a part of the "whole". Studies should take into account the context, the social and natural environment. Everything is connected to everything (Hurtado de Barrera, 2000 p. 149).

ACTIVITY

Using the following enunciative sentences, identify the type of research postulated:

- ✓ The present research is made to solve the problem of defending farm crops from locust attacks. The first step will be to indentify the areas suffering from this plague, explain how it affects farmers and propose a viable solution to save crops.
- ✓ The present study proposes that economic relations in the Mango Valley can only be explained in the context of the history of the Mango people and their faith in Superior Beings. The study intends to explain why the Mango people consider market economy detrimental to their salvation.
- ✓ The present research analyzes the structure of family relations in Mango Valley in the context of Mango culture and their economic relations with the National State. The study takes into account the history and religion of the Mango people, their economical structure and distribution process.
- ✓ The present research is intended to explain family relations of a Mango Valley family during the civil war.
- ✓ The present research proposes to explain the effect of sea water on the digestive system of human beings. The study will be done in the Mango Valley, but expected conclusions are esteemed valid for all people in similar situations.

THEME 3 WORKING WITH YOUR ADVISOR

Your research advisor is there to support you with the process. He or she can make suggestions, give you ideas, and help you with such things as getting access to sources. You are expected to meet with him or her periodically.

Remember to keep a record of each meeting, asking your advisor to write down observations and suggestions in your logbook and to sign it.

- ✓ One of the first things that your tutor will look at is consistency. The idea is to keep you focus on your topic, centered on your objectives or hypothesis, covering all points of your outline. When choosing a topic, you acquire the responsibility to work on the subject. It is not a good idea to jump from one thing to another, or just to forget about your original purpose and do something else. Of course there may be circumstances that force you to change your focus. A huge flood in the Talamanca region may prevent you from doing those five interviews you had promised, and still meet the research deadline. But to change because whatever you are doing may take a bit more effort is certainly not a valid reason.
- ✓ Be faithful to your objectives. Sometimes beginners keep the topic, but simply walk away from their objectives. This too is to take a wrong approach. A research project is designed to carry out the objectives that are laid down by the researcher himself. To devoid from one's self set goals will produce a lousy result, be a personal set back, and may even lead to the discredit of the researcher.
- ✓ Be positive to cover all aspects of the outline. You may add new elements for enrichment, or discretely eliminate a point or two if that action will improve the study. But remember, any change should be consistent with your objectives and also very well justified. The example given above relating to the flood in the Talamanca region is a good example of one reason why you may have to change your outline.
- ✓ Another aspect that your advisor will certainly look at is if you are making good use of your sources and resources. You should maximize their use. Things like basic premises of the research theory, statistics, diagrams, flowcharts, are all of concern.
- ✓ Technical instruments such as questionnaires, lab instruments used for experiments or for testing, samples, tools, computer programs

will be also taken into account. Personal resources—experts, informants, observation of relations. Institutions—documents, services. Books, magazines, other written materials.

✓ Your advisor will also be interested in observing and helping you to cope with unexpected obstacles, and whether you do or do not follow instructions. Part of the reason why you are being trained from an investigative perspective, is precisely to prepare you to face a quickly changing reality, where in many fields it is very difficult to make correct predictions for even a day ahead. In real life you will be facing constantly with the unexpected. The idea is that you will be adequately ready to react to the situation without upset or disruption.

✓ The obstacles you may have to face when doing research may be a source of discouragement. It is the advisor's obligation to point out to advancements and limitations. His or her suggestions are solely intended to better the research. Take them seriously.

✓ Another element to analyze and to promote is your capacity to be selective. Critical thinking is vital to improve your thinking skills and thus better prepare you to succeed in a fluidly changeling environment that constitute today increasingly global society—and this is true in sciences, or any other discipline. When doing your research, not all the information you find will be useful. Some information is basic and pertinent. But some are just not related or inadequate. You must be able to choose properly what information you want to include, what information is directly related to your objectives. Furthermore, sometimes you may run into fallacies, contradictions or simple nonfactual data.

✓ Beware of the questions you make. To ask questions is important, since that is one way to overcome your lack of understanding in a particular field. But, be careful to ask the right person—someone knowledgeable in the field. And make sure that the questions you are asking does not give the impression that you are not doing your part or just trying to find an easy way out.

✓ Finally, time will be considered. Are you using your time wise fully? Sometimes adjustments in the calendar might be necessary due to circumstances out of control. But all effort must be made to live up to your timetable. If changes are needed, discuss them with your advisor. It is not wise to make three trips to the same place, if two is enough.

Your tutor will be checking on your logbook. He or she may want to make an observation in relation to the use of time. This sort of observation sometimes will work against you at evaluation. Keep your record clean.

THEME 4 PREPARING TO DESIGN YOUR TESINA PLAN

Choose a topic of your interest.

It is important when choosing a topic, to select something that is of interest to you. A good undergraduate report will only come as the result of a successful combination of knowledge, experience and your attitude towards the matter. Don't start from absolute zero on this point. Incorporate your interest. Think carefully about what you want to do.

Illustration 2.1: You may want to probe on social concerns.

You will be preparing your undergraduate project and doing the documental research this year. Next year you will complete the job with your field work and prepare your written and oral reports. So you will be investing a lot of time on the matter. It is therefore vital that you choose carefully. You need to be motivated.

Illustration 2.2: You may choose nature.

Define the research problem.

Scientific research stems from a problem. In other words, the reason for doing research is to solve some sort of problem. This means that you must narrow your topic until it becomes more manageable. One doesn't study everything about oranges. You concentrate on one aspect of the orange at a time, ask yourself a question about it, give a tentative answer and then try to prove that your answer is true with supportive data. Coffee is wide. High Mountain Coffee Farms in the Los Santos Region" is more manageable.

To formulate your research problem you have to pose questions that in one way or the other summarize the problem. Exactly, what is the problem to be analyzed in your research? Why do you consider that it is important to resolve the issues that you will be studying in your research? What knowledge do you expect to bring to surface? Where and when will your study be done? Or on what place- time setting will you do your probe? What is the magnitude of your problem? Who is affected by the problem? How will people affected react?

A good definition of your problem is a great starting point to formulate your research hypothesis.

Do a preliminary research

It is cardinal to do a preliminary research. Over the ages, human beings have accumulated a lot of knowledge. In recent years, tons and tons of written pages have been amassed on a number of subjects. There is almost no topic that you can think about that has not been tackled by someone else.

If you go directly into your study without taking a look at existing material on your topic, you may give the impression to your reader, that you are not well informed and may even be exposing yourself to ridicule. Or, you may be repeating a study that already has been done, with the exact same focus. In Spanish there is a saying that illustrates this point:

"A estas alturas no se vale tratar de inventar el agua tibia".

In other words, it is quite too late for you to try to be the inventor of lukewarm water.

Illustration 3: A preliminary research is indispensable

Another related point is that you need to be sure that there are enough sources available. If it is true that most likely there is a lot of information on any given subject, the sources may not be sufficient to do the job.

Even if abundant information is available, it may be in an area where field work can be dangerous. A study on a species of beetle that has been discovered recently, only in a very specific location, might be very attractive to you. But, what if there is only one article on the subject? If there is enough background information, but the beetle is only located in Fiji and you are doing your study for West High in San José Costa Rica, how would you do a field work on this beetle? And if the information is abundant, the beetle located in an area to which you have direct access, but the area is controlled by a violent narcotics band that uses this beetle in the elaboration of a certain weird drug — it might not be wise to study that beetle after all.

Preliminary research is done on the Internet, in libraries, or via conversation with specialists. Search engines such as Yahoo, Google and others are a great starting point. But, information on the Internet is not always accurate. Of course, you can pick and choose, selecting university and other reliable sources. But in any case, the information is useful in the preliminary research stage — it helps you to broaden your knowledge and to have a better perspective of the diverse approaches that might exist on the matter. But, it is wise to corroborate Internet information elsewhere.

One vital source is the library. You don't have to read complete books at this stage. Take a look at the book's table of contents and index. That will give you quick but reliable information about the book's contents, and help you decide if you want to read a portion of the text at this moment, save the reference for later consultation or simple discard the book.

Magazines and articles from specialize encyclopedias are additional sources that you may want to consult.

Don't get lost. You are trying to decide if you are going to stick by your topic; limit it with a certain focus; change it completely. You are looking for available and credible sources to do your work.

Are there enough studies done by other people that will enable you to support your idea, or to provide information to back up your future findings? Remember that you are doing a scientific report. Unsubstantiated opinions of others are of no use. Every part of your work will have to be supported by reasonable arguments and/or data.

Choose a title for your work

Titles are important. They give the reader an idea of what the paper is about. Titles for an investigative report should correspond to the general objective.

Titles don't have to be literal. You can add complementary information, to invite the reader. But don't go too far: your work is an academic report, not fiction.

THEME 5 YOUR PROJECT DESIGN

Decide on the scope of your study

At West, a group tesina is expected. Three members are enough. So, at this point, come to an agreement with your partners, doing your best to comply with the interest of all members of your team.

There are a diversity of possible scopes for your research, depending on the objectives, research strategy, time, and personal interest. Together, they integrate the holistic approach (Hurtado de Barrera, 2000)

First, there are two major divisions: Non-intervention studies and intervention studies.

In the first case, the researcher limits himself to observe and analyze situations or objects. Aside from observing, he does not intervene in the process. In the second case, the researcher manipulates the objects or situations, with the intention to measures the results.

Intervention studies are experimental. The idea is to produce reliable proof that the hypothesis is valid. Experimental researches are very consistent in the use of contrasting samples. One group is exposed to manipulation, while the other is not. The result of the intervention is obtained by comparing the two groups. In the social sciences, the usual practice is to allocate individuals randomly to the different groups. Another type of experimental study uses only one group for the experiment, but there is a pre-analysis of the situation before the intervention and a post-analysis after the intervention to compare effects.

Nonintervention studies are more frequent in social sciences, although the very presence of the observer is to a certain extent an intervention. In the natural sciences, preference is given to intervention studies.

Research can be exploratory

That is, a small-scale study normally applied when there is very little information about a situation or problem. This type of research may look at the problem from different points of view, and if possible, should use as much diverse independent sources to cross check the information. Exploratory studies are used in two cases: to give a quick overview of a situation so that urgent action can be taken, or as prelude to a large-scale descriptive or comparative study. Some sciences, for example astronomy, rely basically on exploratory studies.

Research can be descriptive

Descriptive studies are intended to give a description of the characteristics of a particular event, situation, objects, or case. It is not as wide as an explorative study, but rather restricted to give in-depth characteristics of a limited number of events, situations, objects or cases.

Descriptive researches are used to portray and quantify the object of study, according to the distribution of a set of variables. Such aspects as the prevalence of certain social conduct (at. ex. violence) in a given population; educational levels of a group in relation to their age and income; and to survey political opinions of a sector of population in relation to government systems.

Some descriptive studies are repeated over time to measure changes. For example in an educational program, there can be a pre-survey to assess the situation of the students, and after the course, a post-survey to determine to what degree the program brought about changes. Geography recurs to a lot of descriptive studies—it depicts a lake, a mountain, a volcano and gives us additional information such as the latitude and longitude to locate them.

Research can be analytical and comparative

In this case, the researcher compares two or more events, situations, objects or cases. The author describes each group, looking for aspects that are common to some or to all, but also contrasting differences. A research questions such as "Is there a larger number of single mothers in Puntarenas than in Palmares?" would lead to an analytical probe. The study might compare such variables (aspects to be measured) as educational level, economic problem, family violence, and number of cases of rape in both areas. In addition to describing these variables, the author would also try to determine which socio-economic or cultural factor may be used to explain differences, and even to design a program to combat the situation.

In natural sciences, analytical studies are usually complemented with a control group. If a company is testing a new cream to combat allergy caused by certain type of butterflies, at least two groups would be selected. The new cream would be applied to one group and a placebo (a non-active substance) to the other control or comparison group. Both groups would be exposed to these butterflies for a certain time period, the cream applied to only one, and then the results would be compared to determine whether it is effective or not.

The researcher should be very careful when matching groups. The event, situation, objects, or cases must be similar, as well as the control group; similar, not the same. To compare the level of investment of a Wall Street broker with the level of investment of an isolated aborigine would be a lousy analytical study, to say the least. We don't need a research to understand why poor people "refuse" to buy expensive cars. Examples of good match variables are age with age, source of origin with source of origin, religion with religion. You do not compare religion with printers.

Analytical studies use more complex methodological tools and theories to do comparison. Some sciences such as sociology, relies heavily on analytical studies.

Research can have a theoretical approach

That is, it can be oriented to produce new scientific principles. This is used mainly in philosophy of sciences—epistemology, the theory of knowledge. Epistemology is the branch of philosophy concerned with the nature and scope of knowledge. However, this level of studies is far beyond what is expected in an undergraduate report.

Research can adopt a predictive approach

Prediction is based on the law of probabilities. If you have a set of data that indicates a certain tendency, you can anticipate that if the tendency continues, X or Y results will be reached. For example, when studying population growth, the researcher may have taken a look at changes in a given population over the last fifty years. Looking at the data, he came to the conclusion that the growth rate is 20% per year, because of massive immigration. This has put a lot of strain on the health care system. From his data, he could very well predict that if this tendency continues, sixty additional doctors will be needed in the next five years.

EXAMPLE OF PREDICTION:

Knowing that on planet Gozvi there were moon eclipses in the years 1960, 1971, 1982, and 1993, in what year will the next eclipse occur?

Illustration 4: Planet Gozvi

Predictive studies are very important for planning. They are not simple unsubstantiated speculations or very obvious inferences. On the contrary, they should have theoretical significance or derive directly from the data and study conclusions.

Research can be confirmatory

Confirmatory researches have been in the later centuries the queen of investigation. In effect, it is a phase of holistic research, to the extent that the researcher lances a hypothesis and tries to demonstrate this through his research.

Confirmatory research also involves taking into account experimentation and verification through a rigorous observation.

Research can be evaluative

An evaluative research is done to find out if the objectives of a plan have been achieved or are in progress. The researcher takes into account such factors as objectives of the project or program vis-a-vis, timetable and results, and tries to find clues in relation to possible causes and corrective actions that might be desirable.

Use your preliminary research as background information

Background information demonstrates to the reader that you know what you are talking about. When doing your preliminary research, you collect a lot of information to widen your perspective. Your reader expects you to put your work in the general context of the field, and to see possible connections. If you are doing an experiment, you are expected to be aware of similar experiments conducted on the subject.

In case there is no previous study, or previous ones are entirely different or incomplete, you need to say so.

> ACTIVITY:
> Discuss the scope of your study with your tutor. Having a clear understanding of the scope will help you chose your method, techniques and procedures.
> NOTE: You may want to do this after writing your objectives and hypothesis.

Set up your research objectives

Objectives of a research project enunciate what the researcher expects to achieve by the study. Of course, they derive directly from the problem as was formulated.

Normally, a study uses two levels of objectives: the general objective and the specific objectives.

The general objective states what the researcher expects to accomplish by the study in wide-ranging terms. Specific objectives derive from the general objectives, breaking them into smaller parts, addressing all aspects of the problem.

Be coherent with your topic and objectives, and place them in logical sequence. They should be phrased in operational terms, establishing precisely what you are going to do. Make sure that they are realistic according to your timetable, availability of sources, and accessibility to sources. Always use action verbs that can be evaluated.

Non action verbs such as "to understand" are improper, since to find out if the person understands you would have to carry out a series of additional actions. While an action verb such as "to identify" can be observed directly in the paper: either there is identification or not.

Your report will be evaluated on the basis of your objectives. That's another reason why they should be formulated with care. An error in the formulation of your objectives, may lead to a bad grade even if the contents are excellent.

Ask yourself if the objectives cover all parts of the study in a logical order? Do they sum up in such a way that, if fulfilled, should the study provide the results needed to solve the problem? Are the objectives realistic?

Planning Guide Summary.	
Write your objectives.	You may write a general objective — a description of the main result expected, and then breakdown that general objective into specific objectives that are operational.
Verb suggestions for writing specific objectives (Hurtado de Barrera 2000, p 91)	To explore, to observe, to register, to recognize, to detect. To enumerate, to group, to classify, to define, to characterize To break down, to compare, to contrast, to differentiate, to criticize. To anticipate, to foresee, to propose, to expose, to plant, to formulate, to program, to design, to invent. To apply, to confirm, to verify, to check, to demonstrate, to try. To modify to start, to change, to realize, to detain. To evaluate. To identify, to compare, to value. To adjust, to reformulate.

Formulate your hypothesis

A hypothesis is an explanation for the research problem and a prediction of a relationship between one or more factors. The researcher is assuming that it is true, but it has to be tested.

The most important thing about a hypothesis is that it is an answer to your research problem, assumed to be accurate. Make it very clear and as simply as you can. The standard enunciation is to state that given two factors, A and B, when term A changes, term B changes in a particular way.

Variables

A hypothesis' normally contains an independent and a dependent variable. A variable is an aspect, a characteristic of an object, person, phenomenon or event, subject to variation.

There are two kinds of variables—independent and dependent. The independent variable is the aspect that you change to test the reaction. That is, the factors that influence or cause the problem. The dependent variable is the aspect that changes when you modify the independent variable, in other words, they are the factors affected by the independent variable.

You must justify your hypothesis. What led you to believe that your hypothesis is the right answer to the research problem? The relation with the problem should be very clear. Also, the relation between your variables ought to be formulated in reasonable terms.

A vital step is to write down your hypothesis as part of your project. If you forget to do so, you may find yourself trying hard to recall what where your variables.

ACTIVITY:

If you have not already done so, define the scope of your study. Having a clear understanding of the scope will help you chose your method, techniques and procedures. NOTE: You may want to do this now that you have written your objectives are hypothesis.

Fieldworks Techniques

Considering Ethics

When planning or conducting research, it is very important that you consider Ethics as an essential part of your study. Among the aspects included in Ethics, are the relation between cost and benefit, plagiarism, who is to gain or lose, and above all, respect for human dignity, the environment and life.

- ✓ If your experiment is going to cause harm, you must ask yourself if it is worth it. Researchers must avoid unnecessarily harming people, other living beings, the environment, or property.
- ✓ Don't deceive the participants.
- ✓ Respect for human dignity obliges you to get informed consent to use people in your experiments.
- ✓ Keep people's privacy private and don't expose confidential material trusted to you.
- ✓ Safeguard the environment. The survival of all of us depends on each one of those small steps that we take in favor or against our planet and its living inhabitants.
- ✓ Be cautious when using animals to not cause them gratuitous suffering, especially if the result is not in their benefit.
- ✓ Don't plagiarize other people's work. If you are using information from a source, cite it properly.
- ✓ Avoid the temptation to make up the result so that it complies with your objectives or hypothesis. In Science it is alright to admit that your hypothesis was wrong or could not be proven, provided that you explain why. But to make up a false result is called fraud. And frauds are crimes.

Quantitative and qualitative research designs

Quantitative research design is the traditional form of investigation used by scientists. Physical scientists rely entirely on mathematical and statistical means to measure results. Social sciences have also adopted this form of research, although, as we will explain ahead, disciplines such as education and anthropology also use qualitative design.

Quantitative experiments are done basically in the same format, with minor differences between them. There must be a hypothesis that can be proven mathematically or with statistics. Study groups are chosen randomly — that is by chance. This is essential. A control group is established, to compare the results.

Only one variable should be manipulated at a time. Quantitative researches are designed in such a way that the study can be replicated by others to obtain the same results.

The basic limitation of this kind of studies is that there are only two possible results: the hypothesis is either proven or not proven. There is no possibility for a debatable outcome. For the social sciences this contains a serious problem, since human relations are much more complex.

Qualitative studies do not center on measuring variables. The basic concern is more on studying themes. The variables are identified and used to help explain a problem or reasons for a given phenomenon. Some researchers however will try to discover indicators that make the variables measurable. Qualitative research is used for ethnographic studies; to gain insight in relation to the attitudes, concerns, value systems, aspirations, culture or lifestyles. Public policy makers, political leaders, community activists, depend heavily on qualitative rather than quantitative research design. It is also widely applied in business decisions — introductions of a new product.

Strategies used by qualitative researchers include Content analysis, Case Study, Focus groups and In-depth interviews, among others.

The basic limitation of a qualitative study is that you cannot test the result with the same mathematical and statistical precision.

Depending on your approach, your techniques will vary.

**Illustration 5.1: What sort of ads would catch
female student's attention during elections?**

**Illustration 5.2: How many students participate in student body
election process, according to sex, age and academic level?**

Although you may use these tools with indicators, there will always
be a gray zone. It is not possible to replicate the study and get the exact

same results. What you do get are tendencies, probabilities, arguments that can widen the comprehension of a situation, but not a definite result.

Experimental research

Experimental research is by far the queen of the system. It is used widely in sciences, especially in natural sciences such as Physics, Chemistry, Biology and Medical Research. Social sciences have also incorporated experimental methods to do their work—sociology and psychology to use two examples.

Experimental research recurs to the use of manipulation of the sample and controlled testing. One or more variables are changed to determine their outcome in relation to a dependent variable. A control group is used to contrast results.

The basic idea motivating experiments is to be able to predict results. The researcher has this hunch that there is a cause-effect relation between A and B. He or she then formulates a hypothesis—an explanation, assume it to be accurate and then set out to prove it. The researcher moves on to design an experiment, select a sample group randomly and a control group, and then manipulates the independent variable (A) and observe the effect on the dependent variable (B).

Illustration 6: Lab research is also fieldwork

There are many different strategies that you can use when designing your experiment. For example:

Pre-testing-Post-testing

You may design a pre-test to determine what the condition of the sample is before you do the manipulation. This is important, because if you don't have an accurate assessment of the situation before you introduce changes, there is no way to prove that those changes are the result of your operation.

After you carry out the experiment, you must then apply a post-test, which is basically the same, to provide evidence that there were effective changes.

Control group

Control groups are set up to contrast with the group subject to the experiment. The control group does not receive the manipulation. For example, if you are testing a perfume to repel mosquitoes, you chose two groups. You have to make sure that the same criteria are used to select both of them. Let's say, 10 students chosen randomly in each group. Both will be living in a mosquito infested area for a week. One group will be asked to use the perfume; the other will be given some neutral substance that will not repel mosquitoes. At the end of the experiment, we compare the degree of mosquito attacks on both groups to provide evidence that the perfume was effective.

Repeated measuring

Repeated measuring is done to observe changes over time. If you have a sample group that is subjected to certain conditions for a long time, you would expect changes to occur. What changes can be observed in a child exposed to high intellectual stimulus? Can we change a person's IQ through education? In an experiment like that, we would have to assess the person's IQ before applying whatever strategy we have decided to use. We would then repeat the test periodically according to the time span periods established in our design to generate a better understanding of the matter.

Double-Blind Experiments

In a double-blind experiment, neither the researcher, nor the participants have any clue about which group is subjected to the experiment and which is the control group. This strategy is used to avoid bias on the part of participants and researchers. It is very useful when probing on delicate issues. For example, the person answering the questionnaire may not express his true belief if he considers that his answer could be detrimental to his interests. Or in a case in which an ethnic characteristic is being tested, if the researcher is from that same group he may tend to accommodate the answers, while if he is not from that group he might very well interpret the answer on the bases of his own prejudice.

If the interview is handled by post, and the sample selected randomly, neither the researcher nor the participant will be able to identify each other. Therefore, liberating the test from bias — as much as that be possible.

There are many other strategies used. You may want to do additional research on the matter.

Random Sampling

One cardinal element when designing your experiment is to choose adequate sample groups. Whether you are studying the ant or children in the Sarapiquí plantations, improper sampling will cause serious problems, which sometimes end up disrupting the whole process.

To sample is to select a number of units from the total population. If the total number of population to be studied is small, you might not need to sample. But in larger populations this is indispensable, since it is very difficult to study the total population, as in a census.

The first decision is to establish the criteria to be used in drawing the sample units. Categories such as age groups, sex, profession, place of residence, or people subjected to a certain experience — alcoholics. What is the size of the population, and how many samples will be needed to represent the 100%?

NOTE:
This may seem a very complex matter to you, but there are many statistical norms used by scientists and several computer programs to help decide on samples. Nevertheless, you are not required to use complex technical tools for your tesina, but use good logical judgment in consultation with your advisor.

Random samples are one of the most common used by researchers. In this case, you take into account the total population and then chose your samples randomly. You may make it as simply as getting the complete list numbered and ask someone completely exterior to the research group or participant to select the numbers. For example, if you assign numbers from one to 80 and have decided to do a test on 8 members of the group, you would ask the person to choose 8 numbers and then match them to the list. You could have all 80 names in a box and ask a child to choose 8. Or you could use a computer program to select the sample group. The same can be done with the 8 members of your control group.

Another possibility is to use stratify random sampling. In this case, you first group the sample into categories—age, gender, profession. Once you have these categories arranged, you select from each strata randomly. This is useful if you are interested in distinguishing the dependent variable according to subgroups.

You may also do systematic random sampling. In this case, you have your total sample numbered. For example, you number consecutively the homes in a street from which you plan to collect information. You then chose an integer such as 3. Starting from 1, you would collect information from all homes in an arithmetic progression -3, 6, 9, 12, 15 and so on.

Illustration 7: Procure a distented environment to do your interviews

Using key informants

In the case of qualitative studies, one very important technique is to use key informants to collect information. This is done by in-debt interviews with people who are well-versed on a given subject. For example, leaders in a community, such as the teacher, the religious leader, the president of the local community organization, or the owner of the community store. You can also use this strategy with a given strata of the population, such as school children, adolescents, housewives, fishermen, etc.

You can also use documents. For example, if you are studying the prevalence of violence in the Christmas vacation season, you may decide to consult the newspapers from the 15th of December to the 15th of January, for the last 5 years to make a list of violent deaths, and their causes.

You must bear in mind that key informants are never chosen at random, but rather as the result of a conscious decision. You are choosing the best available informant—a person with knowledge, experience, and goodwill.

Interviews

Social Sciences rely heavily on interrogative techniques (Hurtado de Barrera, 2000, p. 467). This can be defined as a communicative situation between one or more persons, with the objective to collect information for a research. Interviews are one form of interrogative techniques, widely used. It is useful and cheap—all you need is a pencil and paper, or some type of electronic voice recorder or a camera.

You plan your interview with your objectives (and outline) in mind.

There are different types of interviews—structured, non-structured, with open or closed questions.

A structured interview is based on a questionnaire, carefully designed, that is applied to a number of informants. The questions are exactly the same for all members of the sample group.

The questions can be open. In this case the questions are the same, but there is a certain margin for the informant to elaborate on his answer. For example: Why have the Community Store bought all its hardware from Almacén Cerdas?

The answer could be short or long and detailed.

The questions on the contrary could be closed. Again, they are the same for all informants, but the answer expected is short and concise.

For example, is it true that the Community Store bought all its hardware from Almacén Cerdas?

The answer expected is a plain yes or no.

Non structured interviews are planned with a basic initial outline—a list of themes to give an orientation to the conversation, but follow up questions are introduce by the researcher as the conversation unfolds. The researcher is basically expected to motivate the conversation. For example, we have heard a lot about Almacén Cerdas and its relation to our Community Store. What do you know about this relation?

Surveys

Surveys are used to get very precise answers. The informant is given alternatives and asked to choose one. Contrary to interviews, the validity of a survey is to get direct answers, with no additional information.

Surveys are widely used in marketing and in politics. Normally they are directed to a larger number of populations. For example, you want to find out the preferences of 10th grade students in 3 urban high schools in relation to the consumption of beverages. You would have to do a preliminary research to be positive about what are the most common brands. You then elaborate the question in such a way that the informant limits his answer to choose the alternative that you offer.

Example:

Mark in the box beside the brand, which is your favorite beverage:

☐ *Pepsi*
☐ *Coca Cola*
☐ *Té frío Tropical*
☐ *Other*

Another example:
With what frequency do you take part in church ceremonies?

Daily	•
At least once a week	•
Several times a month	•
Several times a year	•
Only on special occasions (weddings, burial, etc.).	•

Focus groups

A focus group is a small group of informants, that the researcher put together to discuss a certain topic, product or situation. The main idea is to have a broad discussion in relation to the point of interest.

Focus groups are normally integrated by 6 to 12 members, chosen according to pre-established criteria.

This technique is useful for example in the following cases:

Brainstorming. As starting point to clarify the problem, or to find solutions for a problem that the researcher has identified.

To discuss the feasibility of an idea.

Illustration 8: Fieldworks are a group effort

To decide between alternatives, as in the case of a symbol or color to be used for a team or when designing a radio/TV ad.

To choose flavors or other characteristics of a product directed to a certain group of consumers.

The researcher must be very precise on the objective of the focus group and what sort of participants is better suited to achieve his or her goals.

The group meets at a pre-set day and time, for a period that varies between one and two hours, in a distended mood. The researcher leads the session, formulating questions, presenting alternatives and asking the group to respond.

The results of focus group sessions are not universally conclusive, since they are based on a very small group. But if the participants are carefully chosen, the ideas, suggestions or recommendations may prove extremely useful.

Recommendations:

✓ Don't argue with the informer. Your role is to get information from the person, not to confront or to change his or her mind. You want to get opinions, not to impose yours. No matter if the information contradicts your objectives or hypothesis, you must record the person's answer accurately.

✓ When doing your interview, be courteous. Be careful when speaking to the person. Find out and use his or her name. Identify yourself.

✓ Explain very briefly what your subject is. You don't have to get into details about your project, just give the basic information.

✓ Listen to his or her answer. It is very frustrating for the informant to get the impression that you are not really paying attention to his response. If when asking question number two, the informer answers also question number four, take note and avoid asking that question again. Repeating the question gives the impression that you are not paying attention and may upset the informer. If you inadvertently repeat the question, add something such as "Oh, I think you already answered that question" If the person spontaneously adds more information, fine, if not, move on to the next question.

✓ Don't manipulate the answers. A manipulative question would be to motivate the question in such a way that the answer fits into your expectations. For example, what is your opinion about the fraudulent relation between the local Community Store and Almacén Cerdas? The word fraudulent is bias. What if the person's opinion is that there is no fraud in this case? A very widely used example to pinpoint the extreme is to ask the person, do you still beat your mom? If the person answers "no", he is admitting "I used to beat my mom but I don't do it any more". If he says "yes" he is recognizing that he had done so in the past and continues to do so. There is no option to negate the accusation.

✓ Don't take up too much time. Don't overwhelm your informant; don't bombard the person with too many questions. In any case, the informer should be aware of the approximate time you need for the interrogation. In a non-structured interview, it is a good idea when ending the conversation to ask the person if he or she has anything more to add.

✓ You must start with courtesy and end with courtesy. Give a hearty thank you to your informant. The person has given time to you, although he had no obligation to do so.

✓ Write down carefully the name of the informant and the place and time when the interview was done. You will need that information when reporting.

Citations (in text)

APA style

All printed, graphic, sound or digital materials consulted should be registered and consigned as resources used.

Below are examples of most common situations that you may encounter.

APA system, is the most commonly used to cite sources within the social sciences. Below are examples of common situations that you may encounter. Suggestions provided are according to the revised 6th edition.

Format for Quotations:
Fisher (1998) observes that for the Akan people "Each human being in community is valuable from birth until death. Even after death, the worth of a human person continues to be respected because the dead person is living on in the community of the ancestors" (p. 65).

Another format for long quotation:
"Each human being in community is valuable from birth until death. Even after death, the worth of a human person continues to be respected, because the dead person is living on in the community of the ancestors" (Fisher, 1998, p. 65).

If the quotation is over 40 words
In this case the quote is presented separate from the main text, without quotation marks:

It is quite interesting that the study was conducted by a Western religious clergyman who lived among the Akan for many years. He observes that among them moral standards are very high. When presenting a child to the community the elder tell the child:

"When you say black, mean black. When you say white, mean white".

In other words, this is the first moral lesson in telling the truth. Since right speech and social sensitivity are very important to the Akan, this ritual contains deep signification. (Fisher, 1998, p. 85).

As observed in Fisher´s text, among the Akans, to become a member of a clan, a person must be honest and hardworking, with high moral standards.

NOTE Use p. for one page and pp. for more than one.

You MUST give citation credit when you directly quote and even when you paraphrase any author's ideas. If you fail to acknowledge your debt to source authors, you are guilty of plagiarism, a serious violation of the law and School rules.

All publication manuals insist that every single reference cited in the text must appear in a reference list, or consigned immediately after the citation, with all data necessary so that a reader can locate the original material.

Single Author

In the body of the paper, use the author's name and the year to identify your source. When referring to an author's idea without a direct citation, you may do this in either way as listed below:

Duncan (2012) denied the post-slavery trauma that some psychiatrist postulated.

Or

The post-slavery trauma was denied (Duncan, 2012) with very forceful arguments.

Two Authors

If the material that you are using was written by two authors, always cite both names (and year) every time. For example: (Kubis & Howland, 1990).

More than one, but less than six authors

If the material that you are using was written by more than two authors, cite names and year the first time that the reference occurs. For example (Casanovas, Molero & Duncan, 2005). After that, you cite only the surname of the first author, and add the expression et al and the year. Example: (Casanovas et al., 2005).

More than six authors

If the material that you are using was written by more than six authors, you only cite the surname of the first author, adding et al and the year from the very first time that the reference occurs. For example, (Landers, et al, 2006).

Take note that in all cases you use only the last name of the author in parenthesis. This should always be so, unless you have two authors with the same surnames, in which case use the initial of their first name to distinguish them. For example: (Peters, B & Peters, W, 2010).

MLA Style

As stated above, it is important to give a complete list of the works consulted in the research process. All printed, graphic, sound or digital materials consulted should be registered and consigned as resources used.

But that is not enough. It is expected that the writer give an exact idea of what he took from each author.

Another way to do so is to use the MLA system. This form of citation is more common in the field of humanities and literature.

The identification of the author and the page number are indicated in parenthesis.

Below are examples of most common situations that you may encounter.

Parenthetical citation

But that is not enough. It is expected for the writer to give an exact idea of what he took from each author. The easiest way to do so is to use the MLA system. The indication of the author and the page number are indicated in parenthesis.

Whether the citation is textual, by paraphrase or even a summary, it is important to mention the author and the page from which you borrowed the idea. If a period is required, place it after the reference (Lawrence 5). Use quotation marks to mark the quotation.

EXAMPLE

> It should be very clear to all beginners that "vocabulary acquisition, vocabulary retention, and vocabulary utilization are crucial for any writer" (Lawrence 5). There is no way to be a writer, if one does not have a broad domain of the language.

If the reader wants to get a better understanding about the source, he can go to the Reference section (bibliography) — the complete list of works consulted at the end of the paper. It is therefore indispensable to include all works cited in the list.

The name of the author could be incorporated in the text itself. It's a matter of style. In this case, only the page number is included in the parenthesis.

> It should be very clear to all beginners, as Lawrence maintains, that "vocabulary acquisition, vocabulary retention, and vocabulary utilization are crucial for any writer" (5). There is no way to be a writer, if one does not have a broad domain of the language.

It is recommendable to make short quotations. But there are cases in which the author needs to incorporate a larger portion of the text. In this case the following MLA rule apply: "If a quotation runs to more than four typed lines, set it off from your text by beginning a new line, indenting one inch" (Gibaldi 73). One inch is roughly 10 spaces.

EXAMPLE

A writer may very well use ideas from other authors when writing. But it is important not to abuse.

> "Quotations are effective in research papers when used selectively. Quote only words, phrases, lines and passages that are particularly interesting, vivid, unusual, or apt, and keep all quotations as brief as possible. Over quotation can bore your readers and might lead them to conclude that you are neither an original thinker nor a skilful writer" (Gibaldi 72).

Gibaldi's advice should be taken into account at all times. The future of a writer may well depend on this.

References

- ✓ Sources cited in your work, if written, must appear at the end of your report.
- ✓ Start your reference list on a new page, headed by the word "References" at the top of the page and go on to enlist the sources used in alphabetical order.

✓ Reference list should be presented in double-space, with a hanging indent format.

✓ Take note that the Authors' names are inverted. The last name is written first, followed by a comma and the first name.

✓ Place your reference list entries in alphabetical order, using the last name of the author or the first author of each work.

✓ In case there is more than one article or book written by the same author, place them in chronological order, from earliest to most recent.

✓ Check further information and examples in THEME 5 REFERENCES.

✓ Observe carefully to see where the commas, colons, periods, and spaces belong.

COMPLEMENTARY SECTION

A Sample Research Project

West College High School

Use of Plants to Treat Skin Problems in An Afro Caribbean
Community.

Ernesto Robinson

Integrated Learning Unit
Advisor Professor Reina Reyes
March 12, 2010

ABSTRACT

Note:
Professional investigations require that the researcher write a small summary of his project. This is called an abstract. Normally, it should not be over 700 words.

ABSTRACT:

There was a backlog of ancestral knowledge in the Afro-Caribbean community in Central America, which has not been validated by science in general, but which has been validated by practices among communities. This ancestral lore consists of asymmetrical traditional knowledge, approaches, spiritual therapies, therapeutic techniques and diverse naturopathic health beliefs inside Afro-Caribbean community in the field of health.

This project aims at documenting the knowledge of medicinal plants traditionally used by the Afro-descendant community of New Line, Limon, Costa Rica, under the premise that there is know-how of these communities on natural remedies for the treatment, prevention and cure of some endemic and epidemic diseases existing in the Caribbean zone and in the country. The enquiry aims to collect a set of such knowledge, and to document it scientifically.

INTRODUCTION

The idea behind this project is that the knowledge on medicinal plants in possession of the Afro Caribbean communities, are at peril, as the older members of the community die out and the younger ones growingly ignore traditional knowledge to embrace mainstream medicine. It is my firm conviction that the bulk of the information on health available in those communities that has been applied to the prevention and cure of diseases can be administered alternatively or complementary.

This knowledge that has been orally transmitted when exposed is done without due recognition, and so, in the eyes of the public at large cease to be the heritage of the Afro-descendant community. Also, as a general rule this traditional knowledge in the field of health, is not known in circles of the official medicine practitioners, and in any case, it does not have the sufficient prestige to win the respectability of the younger people, who opt for a scientific approach alien to their tradition, that do not take into account the specific bio-environmental situation of the Black population.

The importance of the project lies in the conservation of such knowledge to be placed at the service of the new generations. The idea is not only to preserve the findings as if they were parts of a museum of ancient artifacts, rather, the probe is built on the premise that the overwhelming majority of these skills are still valid, and that at best, the natural remedies used in New Line, for the treatment, prevention and cure of some endemic and epidemic diseases may be also useful in other parts of the country. So that the beneficiaries will be in first place the same descendant community, and secondly, the entire national community that will be introduced to these alternative treatments as a means to influence the health of a community that, at least in the rural areas, still see in the natural medicine its first choice.

A background review conducted recently revealed that there is no study of this type done on the subject. What we found were collections of information with a folklorist vision. That is the case of the work of Professor Matthew Vencuez who collected information on the uses of the plant known as Rose of Jamaica (sorrel), in order to create a play. Two studies escape from this categorization: Rosita Arvigo and Michael Balick (1998) on herbal remedies in Belize and Lorena Madrigal's (2006) work on common diseases in the Afro-Caribbean population of Central America.

OBJECTIVES.
GENERAL OBJECTIVES:
To retrieve a body of ancient knowledge on natural health from the Caribbean population of New Line, documenting it scientifically, to put it at the service of the new generations.

SPECIFIC OBJECTIVES:
To identify herbs and medicinal plants of frequent use for the cure of cutaneous affections in the Afro-Caribbean community from New Line.
To document these herbs and plants from a scientific perspective.

TENTATIVE OUTLINE

Introduction
Identification of herbs and medicinal plants.
Popular name for the plant.
Place where the plants were found.
Use of the plant according to informants.
Documentation of the scientific and popular names of the plants identified in that region
Conclusions
Bibliography

RESEARCH PROCEDURES

The line of research is exploratory, and it will lead to the identification of medicinal herbs and plants in the Afro-Caribbean community from New Line. This information on the traditional medicinal knowledge and beliefs will be retrieved through 5 interviews with people who practice traditional medicine in the community. The questionnaire to be applied is designed with a clear and simple language, but which meet standards of validity and reliability.

Interviews will be personal; the interviewer will apply the questionnaire and introduce the questions, with the annotation of the respective answers. In characterizing this research work, by its scope, it will be descriptive, as its central goal is the description of the therapeutic practices based on the information gathered. The data source will be basically the surveys and to a lesser extent, direct observation and photographic documentation. The information collected in the field work, will be transformed into data to be analyzed later in order to obtain the results and conclusions.

RESEARCH CALENDAR

Main Activities	Dates
Interview	March to April
Analysis of data	April
Scientific definitions	May 2-14
Preparing results	May 15 to June 15
Preliminary presentation of the paper	June 17
Corrections	June 18 to July 5th
Public defense of the work	July 15th

BUDGET

Budget in US. $.	Funds required
Visit to the zone	500
Lodging	400
Food	300
OPERATIONAL FUNDS	
Paper for the interviews	100
Paper for printer	75
INCIDENTAL EXPENSES	50
TOTAL PROJECTED COST	$.1375

Planning Guide to Be Used with Tutor

The following guidelines for the presentation of your project, is based on forms used by the European Community.

Planning Guide Summary.	
Title of your project	Make it descriptive
Formulate your problem	Start with a research question. Make a plain description of the topic, clarifying and defining ambiguous or technical terms. Give a clear idea of the setting — the space and time in which the study will be done, or the historical space and time object of the probe.
Justify your proposal	Answer these questions: Why did you choose this topic? Why is this Project important? Who can benefit from the results? How will the project contribute to increase the understanding of the matter?

Planning Guide Summary.	
Give a brief summary of background information	Sum up opinions, conclusions and recommendations formulated by other authors as they relate to your study. What relevant source did you consult while doing your preliminary research? Was there any significant political, social, health problem or any other situation or condition that motivated the study? Or, any event that made you "feel" the convenience or urgency to work on this topic? Do you have prior experience on the subject? Be careful to register your sources. Write down the name of the author of the sources consulted and the year of publication.

Planning Guide Summary. CHECK PROGRESS WITH YOUR TUTOR	
Explain your theoretical framework. Also termed "conceptual framework") (This is optional in the case of your tesina).	According to your study you may have to explain your general theoretical framework. A theoretical framework is constructed on the base of an existing theory that can help you explain the problem. For example, if your topic is to explain race relations in a certain context. When doing your preliminary research you found out that there are two different theories on race:

Race is a fallacy. This thesis is sustained by Ashley Montagu (1965: p. 7). This means that race does not exist.

Races exist, not only as a classification of people based on physical characteristics, but set apart as different species of humanity. Race is everything (Robert Knox: 1850)

In this case you contrast both, and chose one. To which theory will you ascribe? This decision will definitely influence the result, since it will lead you to choose methodology that is in accordance with your concept.

Another example: Your topic is on how to grow better crops in a certain environment. You found out that there are two opposing viewpoints on the subject: those that believe in organic farming, and those that propose transgenic technology. You examine both, explain the difference briefly, state where do you stand on the matter and later choose methodology that is concordant with your theoretical framework.

Planning Guide Summary.	
Diversify your sources	Remember that a project is a PLAN It is always a good idea to consult diverse sources. You will have a wider understanding of your study, and give the future reader the impression that you are versed on the subject. Remember that the Internet is a good starting point, but it is a weak source in the sense that not all the information found online is reliable. The fact is that there are good data bases but also a lot of rubbish. So, use the Internet with a critical eye. Newspapers, magazines, radio interviews, specialized encyclopedias, CDs, DVDs, movies—these are useful when designing your project. Also bear in mind, that the most reliable sources are still books, university dissertations, scientific articles, institutional reports, and interviews with specialist. Of course, experiments are the leading sources. Use tables of contents, indexes; read first chapters, first paragraphs and first lines—in this planning stage your endeavor is to identify sources that you will use later.

Planning Guide Summary.	
Formulate your hypothesis	Your hypothesis is a tentative answer to your research problem, which you are assuming to be accurate but have to test.

Remember that a hypothesis contains variables. A variable is a characteristic of an object, person, aspect, phenomenon or event, which is subject to variation. |

There are two kinds of variables—independent and dependent. An independent variable is the aspect that you change to test the reaction. The dependent variable is the aspect that changes when you modify the independent variable; in other words, they are the factors affected by the independent variable.

For example, if you are going to test a new fertilizer to see how it stimulates the growth of a group of plants, the fertilizer is the independent variable, while the growing plants is the dependent variable, since they will grow slower or faster according to the way in which the fertilizer is administered. In other words, in this case, plant growth depends on the fertilizer.

Make sure that your hypothesis is not a vague or general statement that may not need demonstration. To say that "spheres are round" is true but needs no demonstration. All spheres by definition are round.

But a statement like "if sugar is served daily to a group of rats over a period of six months, they will develop diabetes" is a statement that has to be demonstrated to be accepted as "true" by others.

In this case, there is an independent variable, (feed sugar to the rats) and a dependent variable (getting diabetes).

Planning Guide Summary
EXAMPLES OF HYPOTHESIS

Gasoline consumption in Costa Rica is counter-proportional to its price. Consumption augments over 40% yearly as price increases.

In the community of San Fernando the inhabitants with less educational level, receive the highest income per capita owing to traditional land distribution.

Bird population in San Juan is 30% higher when compared to Cinco de Queso, due to denser native woodland.

The application of the organic fertilizer Foliar Drop every two months determines up to an average 60% increase in size of ferns produce in the Holy Saint Area.

All realistic novels in Costa Rica during the 1940s of the XX Century present confrontation and contrast between rebellious characters and submissive characters in relation to the status quo.

Whenever there is a series of seismic events in the Southern region, there is a 70 to 80% increase in the consumption of flashlight batteries.

Planning Guide Summary.	
Elaborate your tentative outline.	Your tentative outline is an unsurpassable tool to bring order to your work.

A tentative or initial outline is based on the specific objectives, and must be coherent with them. In fact, it should be a complete breakdown of all of the objectives.

Rank them in such a way that the most general points are placed at the heading of each section, and the subordinated points are linked to them with an obvious logical relation between the themes and subthemes.

Do your best to balance these parts or sections, according to the importance attributed to each.

EXAMPLE

INTRODUCTION

1. ADVANCED CONCEPTUAL FRAMEWORK

    1.a Positivism
    1.b Structuralism
    1.c Pragmatism
    1.d Holism

2. REVISING YOUR PROJECT

CONCLUSIONS

Planning Guide Summary.	
Specify your methods, procedures and/ or techniques.	How will the experiment be done? Your methodological section is vital. It must provide a clear, complete and coherent description of the methods and techniques that you are going to use in your research.

Mention scales and other similar means that you intend to use when measuring results.

Justify the experiments you are planning to undertake.

Explain what instruments you will be using to prove your hypothesis or fulfill your objectives.

Describe your research protocol step by step. Remember that the validity of your study depends on the possibility that it can be replicated following the same steps.

And, very important, justify your choice of the particular method and procedures that you are going to use.

If pertinent, details about the people to be interviewed should be included, as well as ideological and ethical considerations related to the study.

Planning Guide Summary

Specify your methods and techniques.	How will the experiment be done?

If your approach is original, be very specific explaining why you are discarding existing methods and adopting your own.

Keep your work coherent with the problem and objectives and cover all of the project's objectives as broken down in the outline.

Depending on the project, the resource section would include some of the following items:

- ✓ Lab protocol, instruments and materials if the study is to be done in a scientific or computer laboratory.
- ✓ Instruments and guidelines for observation.
- ✓ Polling instruments

LAB PROTOCOL

A lab protocol is the standard operating procedure that you will be following to carry out your experiment. It consists of a list of instructions used.

In the future, any other researcher may replicate the experiment and most likely — if conditions are more or less the same, will obtain similar results.

Lab protocols are also written to safe guard from accidents, and to establish proper use of instruments when performing intervention.

Planning Guide Summary.	
Specify your timetable.	Bear in mind that the timetable required does not refer to the plan (Project) but to the research as such. For example, your work might be done over a year or more—from plan to the final tesina defense.

✓   Depending on the project, more or less time will have to be provided for background research, interviews, further data collection, experiments, analysis of findings and report writing.

✓   Also important is that you give consideration to the "What if?" question. What if it takes longer than anticipated to get an interview or to acquire materials? Plans should include extra time for unexpected complications.

✓   Present your timetable in an orderly layout, listing all of your activities in chronological order, indicating who is in charge of each activity and when it should be completed.

✓   Remember to check on approximately when are you expected to hand in your plan and when are you expected to defend your undergraduate paper.

Main Activities	Dates
Interview	March to April
Analysis of data	April
Scientific definitions	May 2-14
Preparing results	May 15 to June 15
Preliminary presentation of tesina	June 17
Corrections	June 18 to July 5th
Public defense of the work	July 15th

Planning Guide Summary	
List your resources and make up your budget.	In this section you lists and describe when necessary, the sources and resources that you intend to use when developing your research. Think about this carefully. Your list should be obviously sufficient to complete the project. Resources could be documents, digital data bases, magazines, periodicals, live interviews, as well as living beings and objects. It all depends on the orientation of your project and the field in which you are doing your tesina Use the "Citation" section of this Manual to list your resources properly.

Budgeting may not be required for your tesina. But if it is, keep in mind what was said when analyzing the ethics behind research.

Take time to do your preliminary research on this matter.

If you need money to do your work, you must make sure that you will have enough to cover your cost. It is not a valid excuse to say, "I didn't complete my work because I ran out of money".

SECOND PART:
APPLYING RESEARCH

THEME 6 A Quick Overview Of Your Project

In part one of the course you designed your *tesina* project, that is, your undergraduate research report. And, according to plans, you have done bibliographic work. You are now expected to revise your project and to do the field work.

Remember your timetable. You do not have much time to do the field part of your research, because of your baccalaureate exam. Do a conscientious revision of what you have done so far. If you have to make adjustments, this is the time to make them. Speak to your advisor.

The following checklist will help you keep on track.

Who and for whom?

This question includes three aspects:

- ✓ With whom? That is, are you working alone or with somebody else? As a general rule, your tesina should be individual. But if you was authorized to do a group work, that's alright.

- ✓ The second part is in whose favor the research will be done. It is an ethical question. Will my research be beneficial to a particular person, company or group? In which case, is that OK? It could be, or could not be. Remember that research should not be detrimental to people, or to the environment. You must cause the lease possible harm, or disruption.

- ✓ The third part is whether or not you have a sponsor. Most researches are sponsored by an institution or company. Again, it might be positive or negative. It depends mainly on what the possible application or use. You must be aware of the fact that, unless there is a previous agreement to the contrary, once you hand in the research you will lose control. The research report will be considered legally the property of the sponsor.

What are the expected results?

This question takes us directly into the objectives and aims of the project. The answer should be a description of the expected results, in the form of a general objective, which you break down into specific objectives.

- ✓ Are your objectives formulated correctly with one operational verb each?
- ✓ You must use action verbs that can be directly demonstrated and evaluated.
- ✓ Also bear in mind that you should chose verbs concordant with the scope of your research. An exploratory research is to observe, register or detect. Not to reformulate. Are you using verbs that correspond to the scope of your research?
- ✓ If you have formulated a hypothesis, this question is also useful. Just recall that a hypothesis is a tentative answer to the research problem. As far as the research is concerned the answer is true—although yet to be tested and confirmed.

The next question is: how are you going to do your research?

- ✓ This involves the conceptual framework, the methods, techniques and procedures that you will be using in the research. Read these sections carefully. Give it a last thought.
- ✓ Do you think that it covers all aspects, now that you have done your documental exploration?
- ✓ It is also important to be very clear in relation to the type of method you are using. Keep it coherent at all times. If your project is quantitative, use quantitative methods. If it is qualitative, use qualitative methods.

Next very important question is: where and when (or about what place and time) are you doing your research?

It could a physical or cultural environment. It could be present time or some past time. It doesn't matter. You must indicate time and space.

- ✓ Have you done so?
- ✓ Is the time and place for your fieldwork properly established?

✓ Did you set up a realistic timetable?
✓ Are you sure you don't have to make adjustments?

With what means will you do your research?

Your sources and resources should be sufficient, available and coherent with your project.

Do you have access to the data that you need?

If you need money, do you have enough to carry out your project to the very end?

Ask yourself these questions.

What if?

You should have an alternative plan for each step.

What if something happens and you cannot get to the region on time?

What if the lab cancels your permit to do the experiment?

THEME 7 Collecting Data

Observations

To observe, in a scientific project, is to apply your senses intentionally to a group of objects, phenomenon or people. The observation starts with the observer, and at the end returns to him. The observer is the researcher himself.

Systematic observation is not simple. To observe, the researcher must be trained. He or she of course is using the senses to perceive images, temperature, textures or to capture sounds. But these images are being observed by a person who has his own analytical and reactive mindsets. As we have discussed in former stages of the Learning to Apply series, we all elaborate reactive mind circuits that interfere with our appreciation of reality. This interference is both in the process of collecting data, as well as when processing the information collected.

For example, if we have chosen to interview people from each 5th home of a street block, but when approaching the home we get a "feeling that the situation is dangerous", we may then decide to skip that home. But if we do this repeatedly, it is quite possible that we end up with a complete falsification of results.

Illustration 9: **Careful observations will render better results**

Sometimes we may be tempted to act on the basis of one of those erroneous conclusions or prejudices that we store up in a "ready to use fashion". For example, it is a common saying in Spanish that "siempre que pasa igual, sucede lo mismo".

This, of course, is not true. How many times have we done the same things and do not obtain identical results? This is a very reactive conclusion and it tends to color human relations in a very negative way.

Illustration 10: **Minimize reactive thinking**

On the other hand, if we are monitoring changes in a group of plants, and are supposed to make our observation daily at the same hour, but get into a fit and decide that we are sick and tired of the matter, skip a day or two and later try to reassume our study, the results might not be as precise as we intended.

The above sums up to two points:

✓ You must use a satisfactory instrument that minimizes reactive interference in your study.
✓ You must be systematic and constant when applying your research method or techniques.

Bear in mind, always, that you are part of the reality that you are observing. Your presence is a modifier. For example, if you are participating in a research relating to family relations, and want to register directly how mothers treat their children in a particular social group, it is quite possible that the attitude may be different if the person is aware that she is being observed. This means that you have to be very discreet, avoiding projecting reactive mind prejudice and emotions when doing your work.

Tables

You may use a table to collect and organize your data. Tables will help you show variation in data. This is not a dogma — there are cases in which tables may not apply.

Again, tables are based on the project objectives and correspond to points of the outline.

If you use tables in your report, take into account that they are not a substitute for text. What you can do is number your table and refer to it in the text.

Searching for medicinal plants, you may find several in the area that you are studying. Your interest is to identify the plant and its use.

Your table might look like this:

NAME OF THE PLANTS			
Popular	Scientific	USE	INFORMANT
Guava	Psidium guajava	For gum bleeding	Pedro Cyrus
Corn	Aea mays	(hair) for urinary retention	Miss. Berta
Lemmon grass	Cymbopogon citratus	For fever and flu	John Castro.

Content Analysis

Content analysis is one of the most useful techniques to perform an exploration of texts and for the observation of movies, radio or TV programs. It allows you to measure the frequency and intensity with which a concept appears, or the specific characteristics of a message.

To implement this technique, you first select the sample material and then proceed to establish in advance the analytical categories.

For example: How to prepare the natural remedies identified in field study?

In the following example, the text used is Farmacopea Vegetal Caribeña, pp. 44-45 and Curación con las plantas medicinales pp.10-11.

The categories are set up in a table:

| Remedy for | Ingredients | Preparation | Application |

After reading the text and extracting the information, your table might look like this:

Remedy for	Ingredients	Preparation	Application
Baldness	10 pieces of mint root.	Cook for 15 minutes in a liter of water.	Use to wash hair twice a week.
Strengthen hair.	Horsetail, rosemary and chamomile	Cook together	Use to wash hair frequently
Source: Curación con las plantas medicinales pp.10-11			
Baldness	Aloe Vera	Liquefy	Use to Massage scalp
Baldness	Potato	Crush	Apply on scalp
Source: Farmacopea Vegetal Caribeña, pp. 44-45			

As seen, in this case it is a quantitative analysis based on the questions of how many times remedies for the hair appear in the texts, which ones and how they are prepared and used.

This technique is also very effective to study hidden messages. For example, if you would like to know to which audience TV programs are directed to on weekdays from 6 PM to 7 PM. One source of information would be to watch the ads. So you set up your table, with the categories you want to use.

For example you may want to use age groups. With that in mind you watch a different TV channel each day from 6 to 7 PM and register the ads, the frequency of advertisements targeted to one sector or another.

Your table might look somewhat like this:

Hour	Day	Channel	Product announced	Characters in the ads (mark with an X)		
---------	---------	---------	---------	Children	Teenagers	Adults
			TOTAL Percentage			

THEME 8 GENERAL CONTENT OUTLINE FOR YOUR TESINA

Revise your paper. These are things you will want to take into account:

Formalities:

- ✓ A front page is required.
- ✓ You may dedicate the tesina to someone or to a group, or you may want to use an outstanding citation from some famous author. Make sure that the text used is short and related to your topic.
- ✓ Paper should be 8 ½ by 11 inches (21.59X27.94 cms).
- ✓ Use white paper, preferably bond 20.
- ✓ Leave 1 inch margins on all sides of your paper.
- ✓ Paragraphs should be indented five spaces / roughly ½ inch).
- ✓ Print on one side of the paper.
- ✓ Research papers must be printed double-spaced, including quotations.
- ✓ Pages should be numbered. If you use a title page, number should be omitted on that page, but the second page should be numbered 2 and consecutively right through the report.
- ✓ Research papers must be bound. Make sure this is properly done.

Structure:

Include a table of contents. It could be something like this:
Introduction.
Chapter 1. Background information.
Chapter 2. Methodology techniques and procedures used.
Chapter 3. Presentation of your arguments. Include data, tables, and graphics.
Conclusion. Discussion of the results.
References. Books and other sources consulted.
Annexes (if necessary).

Introduction

The introduction should be no more than 3 pages
Present the problem as you did in the project (research plan).

✓ Include the research question.
✓ Include your research objectives or hypothesis.
✓ Justify the investigation that you have undertaken. Now that you have done the work, you may want to add or do a broader justification. Tell the reader about the importance of what you have discovered, or the possible application of your findings. Be brief.
✓ Describe the place and time that you studied, or when and where the study was done.
✓ Give a quick summary of your methodology. Don't go deep into details if you are going to have a chapter dedicated to methodology. Just mention basics.
✓ It is appropriate to tell the reader whether your study is quantitative or qualitative.
✓ Give a very brief description of what is included in each chapter.

Body of the paper

Chapter 1: Background information
Mention the sources used in the construction of your report. You do not have to mention every source consulted. In fact, if you did a good job, you would have to write a book-length report to include everything. Chose a few that are pertinent. Discuss the material—what was acceptable to you according to your theoretical framework, and what was rejected along with the reasons.

Chapter 2: Methodology, techniques and procedures used.
In this chapter, you give detailed information as to how you did your research from the theoretical point of view.
Begin by establishing the scope of your study. Is it an intervention or a nonintervention study?
Was your report exploratory?
Did you propose a small-scale study intended to collect data on a subject about which little information was available?

Where you trying to give a quick overview of the situation so that urgent action could be taken, or as prelude to a large-scale descriptive or comparative study?

Was your study of a descriptive nature? Did you intend to give a description of the characteristics of a particular event, situation, objects, or case?

Are you going to portray and quantify the object of study, according to the distribution of a set of variables?

Was your research analytical and comparative? Are you comparing two or more events, situations, objects or cases? Are you describing aspects that are common to some or to all, but also contrasting differences?

Does your research have a theoretical approach? That is, was your analysis oriented to produce new scientific principles?

Was your research done with a predictive approach? Are you using the law of probabilities? Were you planning to come to an inference or deduction that could be used to anticipate future result?

And finally, was your research evaluative? Were you examining a group of data or a situation to find out if the objectives of a plan were reached? Was your intention to recommend corrective actions?

Of course, the type of method, techniques and procedures used depended on whether your research was quantitative or qualitative. Explain your conceptual framework. Describe the sample used or type of informants contacted, and what procedures were applied to select the sample or group of informants. Mention the amount of samples or informants used in the study. Give a complete account of the instruments used in the study. Did you use questionnaires, tests, experiment?

Chapter 3: Presentation of your arguments. Include data, tables and graphics.

When writing this chapter, take special care to start each paragraph with a topic sentence. Then add supportive paragraph when necessary. Of course you may do otherwise, but it is better to stay on the safe side. As you develop practice you will be able to go beyond these recommendations, be creative and still keep your status as a respectable writer.

Supportive sentences are written to expand on the main idea, to give more information to endorse your main idea. In this section use the information that you collected wisely.

Internally, each paragraph should have a main idea and if necessary supporting ideas. But the same is true about this whole chapter. You will have paragraphs that explain your main ideas and paragraphs that support those ideas. These paragraphs give examples, arguments and definitions.

- ✓ Argue wisely.
- ✓ Use comparisons — similitude and contrast.
- ✓ Discuss cause-effect relations.
- ✓ Give clear convincing examples.
- ✓ Use analogies.
- ✓ Make well-grounded predictions.
- ✓ Use logical inferences.

All these paragraphs together lead to prove your hypothesis or carry out your objectives.

You link paragraphs together with transition words that help the reader connect them to the thesis paragraph. Transition words make your essay easier to read. Use them at the beginning and end of your paragraphs.

Transition words and phrases

If you wish to be a writer, write. Epictetus

Using transitional words and phrases helps papers read more smoothly.

They provide logical organization and understandability and improve the connections and transitions between thoughts

A coherent paper allows the reader to flow from the first supporting point to the last.

Transitions indicate relations, whether within a sentence, paragraph, or paper.

This list illustrates "relationships" between ideas, followed by words and phrases that can connect them.

Addition:
also, again, as well as, besides, coupled with, furthermore, in addition, likewise, moreover, similarly

Consequence:
accordingly, as a result, consequently, for this reason, for this purpose, hence, otherwise, so then, subsequently, therefore, thus, thereupon, wherefore

Generalizing:
as a rule, as usual, for the most part,
generally, generally speaking, ordinarily, usually

Exemplifying:
chiefly, especially, for instance, in particular, markedly, namely, particularly, including, specifically, such as

Illustration:
for example, for instance, for one thing, as an illustration, illustrated with, as an example, in this case

Emphasis:
above all, chiefly, with attention to, especially, particularly, singularly

Similarity:
comparatively, coupled with, correspondingly, identically, likewise, similar, moreover, together with

Exception:
aside from, barring, besides, except, excepting, excluding, exclusive of, other than, outside of, save

Restatement:
in essence, in other words, namely, that is, that is to say,
in short, in brief, to put it differently

Contrast and Comparison:
contrast, by the same token, conversely, instead, likewise,
on one hand, on the other hand, on the contrary, rather,
similarly, yet, but, however, still, nevertheless, in contrast

Sequence:
at first, first of all, to begin with, in the first place, at the same time,
for now, for the time being, the next step, in time, in turn, later on,
meanwhile, next, then, soon, the meantime, later, while, earlier,
simultaneously, afterward, in conclusion, with this in mind,

Summarizing:
after all, all in all, all things considered, briefly, by and large, in any case,
in any event,
in brief, in conclusion, on the whole, in short, in summary, in the final
analysis,
in the long run, on balance, to sum up, to summarize, finally

Diversion: by the way, incidentally

Direction:
here, there, over there, beyond, nearly, opposite, under, above, to the
left, to the right, in the distance

Consult Web guidelines. Among these, The Gregg Reference Manual,
The Brief English Handbook, The Least You Should Know About
English
http://www.studygs.net/wrtstr6.htm Online 1/22/2010 7:51:32 PM

Linking to the guides is encouraged!

Using analogy

You may also want to use analogy to argue. Analogies are indirect
affirmation on a subject. Analogies are figurative comparison, and are

not considered a definite proof for anything, but they are useful tools to illustrate a point.

The word is taken from Greek, meaning correspondence, similarity. For example:

- ✓ Far is to near as quick be to slow.
- ✓ Zippers are to shirts as laces are to boots.
- ✓ A people without history are like a tree without roots.
- ✓ Anorexia is to food as alcoholics are to liquor.
- ✓ East is to west as north is to south.
- ✓ Babies are to humans as puppys are to dogs

Avoid using fallacy

If you use fallacies as arguments, your paper will lose credibility.

The word fallacy is used at times, as equivalent to the "false". In some contexts it denotes a false belief or an error expressed in a statement, but this is a misuse. Of course there is some degree of falsehood in the term, but it is not exactly a synonym. Fallacy refers to "apparent argument" or in other words an illogical argument.

The following are commonly used fallacies:

Argumentum ad baculum (Appeal to force). This type of fallacy alludes to the use of means of coercion; these statements are made to substantiate a conclusion by intimidation.

The following phrase sums up this idea: "force makes the right".

EXAMPLE: *Now, take your pills. I know what is good for you. If you don't, forget about going to Puerto Viejo!*

The reason given to take the pills is coercive—if you don't you will be punished.

<No discussion on this point. It's either do or die>.

In this case, the person is not even listening to the argument. His point of view will be imposed no matter what.

Argumentum ad hominem. In this case, the attack is directed to the person. In other words, instead of trying to refute the truth of what was said, the contender attacks the person who made the statement. The dispute is redirected to cast doubt on the plausibility and/or the consistency of the person.

EXAMPLE: *Your argument in favor of Ms. Garment is not acceptable. We all know that you are defending her because she is a woman.*

Your statement that it is not OK to eat pork is based on the fact that you are a Jew.

These are false premises. The person could have very good arguments to substantiate his or her findings. The contender should oppose arguments with counter arguments, not attack the person.

Argumentum ad ignorantiam. This fallacy is used to affirm or negate an argument on the sole bases that it has not been proven—ignorance. The debater states that so or so is true and when challenged, recurs to the argument that whoever does not agree should prove him wrong. This fallacy is very common in discussions about the possibility of extraterrestrial life.

EXAMPLES: *There are no such things as extraterrestrial beings. Show me one!*

I admit that Marva had a terminal cancer and is now cured. But according to you she was cured by faith. To me that's nonsense. Prove it!

In both cases the person put the burden of proof on the contender. But the fact that you cannot prove something does not lead to the conclusion that it does not exist. Long before they could prove it, people knew that the form of the Earth is like a sphere.

Argumentum ad misericordiam. This fallacy seems to be very popular among students. The appeal is on mercy. The person recurs to compassion to get away with his postulate.

EXAMPLES: *You should condone Tracy's test. She was very nervous last night, because of a family discussion. She woke up with a terrible headache.*

Tracy's health problem, may be sufficient to ask the teacher to have her take the test a little later or another day, but there is no logic in the petition to condone the test. Everybody has family discussions and headaches.

Don't judge my client for his crime. He suffered the same when he was a child.

This argument is not valid. The fact that a person was victim of a crime does not give him the right to commit crimes.

Argumentum ad populum. The debater in this case recurs to the "everybody" argument. As a general rule, politicians use this fallacy a lot.

EXAMPLE: *The film shown last night is of low artistic value. None of those who attended the exhibition liked it.*

The fact that none of the assistance liked the movie is no proof that it is of low quality.

"Obviously, we the people are in total opposition to your thesis. Nobody before you has ever made such a crazy proposal".

Maybe there was no such proposal beforehand because it never occurred to anyone. But that is no proof that people are opposed to the new initiative.

Argumentum ad verecundiam. The argument in this case is based on the premise that something is true because it was stated by an authority.

EXAMPLE: *Aristotle stated that some people are born slaves. I think that that explains the conduct of the Taringas.*

Xincamba lose the gulf tournament. This is a logic consequence of his race. As B.C. Wallace wrote in his extraordinary essay on human races, gulf is too intellectual to be played by members of the inferior races.

These arguments are based on the premise that if a "great thinker" as Aristotle or B.C. Wallace said so, it could not possible be wrong.

So be positive that your arguments are reasonable, convincing, and logical.

Concentrate on your topic, avoiding side arguments and non-related details, no matter how attractive they may seem.

Facts and opinions

Another very important point is not to mix up facts and opinions. Facts are events verifiable by all who take a look with the same approach. Opinions are personal views that are not necessarily counter checked.

For example, *the dog is dead*. If we have the definition that being dead is not breathing, and if the dog is not breathing he is dead.

In contrast, *the dog is beautiful* it is an opinion because we all have different definitions of what is beautiful.

If we say, *this singer was born in Turkey Point* it is a fact. We know the person's origin. Anybody in doubt can go to the civil registry and get a birth certificate.

But to say, *nothing so good can come from a town with the name Turkey Point* is an opinion—a rather prejudice opinion, by the way.

Careful Analysis

Logical Analysis Exercises

a. Place the numbers 4, 6, 2 and 8 in the grid so that in all the columns and rows they add up to 20.

...	...	...	...
...	...	...	...
...	...	...	...
...	...	...	...

b. Place the numbers 1, 2, 3, and 4 in the grid, four times each. Place them in such a sequence that the opposite corners match.

....	...	....	....

c. THE TRICK OF THE COINS. Modify the cross. Move ONE coin to form a perfect cross so as to count 6 coins in both rows and columns.

	.....	Ⓟ	.....	.....
		Ⓟ		
.....	.....	Ⓟ	.....	.....
Ⓟ	Ⓟ	Ⓟ	Ⓟ	Ⓟ
.....	.....	Ⓟ	.....	.....
.....	.....	Ⓟ	.....	.....

d. HIDDEN MESSAGE. I was born after the independence of Costa Rica that was in 1821 and before the years of the great winds (2000). In what year was I born?

Look for the sequence of numbers in the box. There is only one possible.

7	9	9	9	9	9
9	2	0	0	6	9
1	1	9	4	8	8
6	3	3	3	3	9
1	8	2	0	0	9

e. SEQUENCES. In accordance with the data, which numbers correspond to each blank space?

2,3,1,4,5,1,6,7 __

6/3, 5/3, 6/3, 4/3, 6/3, 3/3, 6/3, __/__

2/3, 6/3,18/3 __/3

2/8, 2/6, 2/4 __/__

12/5, 24/4, 48/3, __/__

f. ATM pin.

You forgot the pin number of the ATM machine. Since you have been a forgetful person throughout your whole life, you have come up with a system to remember your pin. Your pin begin with four and combines the lower numbers in sequence (3,2 and 1). You have two possibilities. You first marked

FIRST MARK: 4 3 2 1 Pin wrong.
Which of the remaing possibilities is correct?
4312, 4231, 4123.
If you mark two errors the machine will retain up your card.

Conclusion: Discussion of the results

Make your conclusion is short. Two pages may be more than enough. In any case, don't run over 20% of your complete work.

The idea is to stress the point that you are delivering whatever you told the reader that you would. In other words, after presenting your data and arguments in the body of the paper, you recap the basic ideas in a summary.

You should emphasize consequences and implication of your findings; give recommendations for further research or action; stress the importance and potential use of the results.

THEME 9 A Sample Research Paper

Introduction:
What if, that day when you or a member of your family had sunburn, you could have accelerated healing or avoided the burn using verbena? This study recognizes that there is a good number of traditional knowledge that has been part of the lore of Afro-Caribbean peoples and that over the years. This has been applied as alternative and complementary medicine, both for prevention and cure.

The general objective of the study is to recuperate a body of ancestral knowledge pertaining to natural healing of the Caribbean population of the New Line Village, document it scientifically, and thereby put it at the service of the new generations. This is precisely the importance of the project—the possibility to preserve and past on the information.

But, the idea to preserve is not to set up a sort of museum or ancient knowledge reservoir. As we have demonstrated in the study, the point is that the vast majority of these remedies are still very valid and usable, and that it is quite realistic to postulate that they can be applied successfully to many epidemic or endemic diseases for both prevention and cure.

Our examination of background literature on the subject, led us to conclude that there is no specific study done on the area. There are a few documents with information on the subject but they are designed as part of tourist guide information. Such is the case of the work of Professor Mateo de Jesùs Vencuez, whose main concern was to create a play, using traditional beverages as part of his scenery. He did a very interesting job on the so called China root.

Two studies or not oriented by a folkloric viewpoint—Lorena Madrigal's study on frequent ailments of the Afro-Caribbean population in Central America, and Rosita Arvigo and Michael Balick's study on traditional medicine in Belize. But these studies do not center on the information available in New Line.

Six in-depth interviews were done, among them one with professor Blumenthal, who although not native of the zone, has lived there for a number of years and has done extensive scientific research as well as practical experience in the field of herbology.

This study is descriptive. Its main objective is to depict certain therapeutic practices of the region on the bases of the information identifies and to document the use of three plants used to treat skin ailments.

The sources of the information presented is in a large proportion the interviews, and at a limited degree, direct observation. Scientific documentation is used to support and give a more accurate description of the plants.

THREE TOP SKIN REMEDIES

2.1 Aloe Vera.

Aloe Vera, also called sábila locally, is a thick, dented long-leaf plant that produces small bunches of yellow flowers. The plant is green and it grows roughly to 60 centimeters.

Information on Aloe Vera was provided by 3 of the 6 informants. All 3 agreed that this is the best plant to treat the skin.

Miss Bull, for example, considers Aloe Vera as an exceptional treatment for alopecia (baldness). She also uses it for rare marks that are formed on some mothers belly after childbirth. In both cases, Miss Bull crushes the leaf, and prepares a creamlike application.

Mr. Burns added that it is by far the best treatment for skin burns. He says that he has always used it in his therapeutic practice, and mentions the case of a child with severe burns, who, treated solely with Aloe Vera, had no scars or blemish at the end of the treatment.

Mr. Castrillo mentioned in the interview that in addition to being very effective for baldness and burns, he has used Aloe Vera to extract thorns embedded in the feet.

The following table is a summary of the setting, use, preparation, application and scientific information for Aloe Vera.

SETTING	USE	PREPARATION AND APPLICATION	SCIENTIFIC INFORMATION
Native to Africa and the Mediterranean grows in arid areas but needs abundant irrigation (Rodríguez Navas 161)	Alopecia	It is liquefied and rubbed on the scalp	Scientific Name: Aloe Vera. It has been widely studied. This plant has many biological and chemical properties. Used in many other diseases.
	Burns	The pulp is more or less liquefied and applied on the burn without rubbing or scratching the wound	
	For thorns	The spot should be clean. Then apply Aloe Vera and cover it with a cloth band. The thorns will be expelled gradually.	

2.2 Potatoes

The second plant selected was potatoes. Potato plants are multiple an erect stems, colored green and purple. The tuber is used to prepare allergenic medicine.

Mr. Castillo said that the plant is especially useful for skin allergies and burns. Miss Alfredita agreed, but added that the real effectiveness of the plant is seen when used by on children with a very irritable skin: "Those that don't do well in the bush".

SETTING	USE	PREPARATION AND APPLICATION	SCIENTIFIC INFORMATION
Native of Peru. Produced in template areas all over the world. It is not produced in New Line, but rather brought from Cartago. (Rodríguez Navas 143)	Skin allergies, skin irritation, burns.	Fresh potato juice. This is obtained by blending the potatoes in a bit of water. The juice is applied directly on the skin.	The scientific name of the plant is Soanum tuberosum. It is a well studied plant, especially for its value as food.

2.3 Vervain (verbena)

Vervain is a dark green plant with few stems and leaves. It grows up to 1.5 meters in high.

Usually both leaves and stems are used in the preparation of the remedy. Francisco Cheldon uses it on sunburn cases. He said that is very effective because it is very refreshing.

Miss Bull considers that it is the best for the body pains (neuralgia) and skin irritation caused by exposure to sunlight. People going to the beach should always carry a bottle of verbena, she said. Georgina Blumenthal, although of European origin, has lived for a long time in the area, and has done much study on this plant. She did not hesitate to confirm that vervain is very effective on sunburn and infections.

SETTING	USE	PREPARATION AND APPLICATION	SCIENTIFIC INFORMATION
Vervain is common in all of The Americas. It is abundant in the garden and yards in New Line.	Skin allergies, skin irritation, sunburns Superficial pains, infections.	3 pieces of the plant, including leaves (roughly 15 centimeters) are boiled in 3 cups of water for 15 minutes. It is left to cool. The patient should drink a cup with each meal. The leaves are used for therapeutic plasters.	Scientific name: Verbena litorales.

3 FINAL THOUGHTS

As it has been highlighted in the course of this study, there is a wealth of information in traditional Afro-Caribbean communities on natural medicine. This has proved effectiveness in curing diseases of the skin.

On the basis of the interviews with five informants who are dedicated to administering natural remedies to their fellow citizens in the community of New Line, and a sixth interview with a scientist, we have been able to identify specific treatments used to treat skin aliments.

We have documented three examples of this knowledge about the use of medicinal plants, demonstrating that the people of these communities have natural remedies for the treatment, prevention and cure of some endemic and epidemic diseases, applicable not only in the Caribbean area but also in the rest of the country.

The study draws to the attention of scholars this branch of medicine that has not been given the relevance that it deserves.

It is a fact that for many of the inhabitants of the area, natural medicine is the first option when sick. The official medicine is costly and sometimes not so accessible. But in any case, it is a fact that people rely on traditional medicine as their first choice, and only goes to the doctor if the natural treatment does not provide relief in a reasonable time.

A better understanding and systematization of these natural remedies could help the community to use these remedies with less risk of intoxication.

References (Bibliography).

Arvigo, Rosita y Michael Balick. Rainforest Remedies. 2nd. Ed. USA: Lotus Press, 1998.

Cheldon, Francisco, Farmer. Interview held on April 2nd 2010.

Blumenthal, Georgina, Biologist. Interview held on April 12 2010 at her home.

Germonsén-Robineau, editor. Farmacopea Vegetal Caribeña. 2da. Ed. UNAN-León, 2005.

Madrigal, Lorena. Human Biology of Afro-Caribbean Populations. USA: Cambridge, 2006.

Pen Pen, Alfredita. Teacher. Interview held on April 11, 2010 at her school.

Mamá Bull. Houswife. Interview held on April 13, 2010 at her home.

Rodríguez Navas, Hernán. Utilidad de las Plantas Medicinales. Heredia, Costa Rica: EUNA, 2000.

Castrillo, Ossi. Herbal Therapy. Interview held on April 14, 2010 at his home.

Burns, Gigi. Administrator. Interview held on April 9, 2010 at his grocery shop in New Line.

THEME 10: References

- ✓ Remember reference rules.
- ✓ Books and magazines and newspapers cited in your work, if written, must appear at the end of your report. Start your reference list on a new page, headed by the word "References" (Bibliography) at the top of the page and go on to enlist the sources used in alphabetical order.
- ✓ Reference list should be presented in double-space, with a hanging indent format.
- ✓ Take note that the Authors' names are inverted. The last name is written first, followed by a comma and the first name.
- ✓ Place your reference list entries in alphabetical order, using the last name of the author or the first author of each work.
- ✓ In case there is more than one article or book written by the same author, place them in chronological order, from earliest to most recent.
- ✓ Be aware of the fact that APA reference system no longer requires quotations marks, italics or underlining of the title of book or articles.
- ✓ In the following examples, observe carefully to see where the commas, colons, periods, and spaces belong.

APA Style

Electronic Sources

Some sources online may not be accurate. For example, Wikis and other collaborative projects cannot guarantee the verifiability or expertise of their entries, and for that reason, the information is not acceptable as conclusive data or proof for your research. So when using these sources, make sure that you double check information by other means.

When citing a source online, use the following format;
If the source is signed:
Murillo, Sandra. (October 19, 2009), "Estudio que de un panorama general sobre la situación en Centro América".Guatemala: Incap. Retrieved from http://www.depadresahijos.org/INCAP/Obesidad.pdf

Unsigned article:
El Universal.com(October 19, 2009). "Padres obesos, hijos con sobrepeso". Retrieved from http://www.eluniversal.com.co/cartagena/vida-sana/padres-obesos-hijos-con-sobrepeso-25095
You must give the complete citation the first time. After that, use only the author's last name, or the first author's last name and the year.

Music recording.
Jackson, Michael. (2010). The Essential Michael Jackson. [CD]. EU: Sony Music.

Motion picture.
Río Nevado Producciones (Producer), Ross, Yasmín. (Screenwriter) Luciano Capelli (Director). (2000). El Barco Prometido [Motion Picture]. Costa Rica: Río Nevado Productions
Videocassette/DVD

Byrne, Rhonda and Harrington, Paul. (Producers), Heriot, Drew. (Director), v. (Writer), (2006). The Secret [DVD]. Australia: Prim Time Productions.

A Radio or Television broadcast.
González, Rodolfo. (Producer). (2012, November 1). 7 Días [Television broadcast]. San Jose: Teletica.

Ibarra, Vilma. (Producer). Hablando Claro. (2009, December 6) [Radio Broadcast] San José: Radio Columbia.

Personal Communication:
Some materials such as e-mails, messages from electronic bulletin boards, non-published interviews and telephone conversations are considered personal communications, and should only be cited in

the text (not in the final reference list). Nevertheless, a precise citation is required. Full names or initials and surname of the communicator and the exact date of the message or interview should be included.

For example:

C. Delgado (personal communication, August 12, 2012) suggested changes in the order of the book.

Or,

Suggestions of changes in the order of the book were made earlier in the year (C. Delgado, personal communication, August 12, 2012).

An interview.

Pedriarias, D. (2011, June 2). Personal interview.

Encyclopedia.

Mascare, U and Solac, B. (Editors.). (2002). The Modern Guide to Alternative Medicine. (3rd ed., Vols. 1-19). New Hopeville: Ocean Wave Editions.

An article from a printed magazine.

Bonansku, José. (2012, January 11). Autism Today. Revista Dominical, 17 (3), 11-14.

Graduate dissertation. (Thesis)

Oses Cordero, Guillermo Emilio (2001). In Search of the Lost Paradise. Unpublished doctoral dissertation, Universidad Nacional.

MLA Style

Books published prior to 1900.

Older books that were published before there was a convention as to what information should be included for reference, may not comply to modern standards. Some data may be omitted or consigned in a simpler way. The name of the publisher may be omitted and commas may be used instead of a colon.

Sufe, Carl. Prussia under War. Italy, 1897.

Books published after 1900.

Author (Last Name, Name). Title. Place: Publisher, year.

EXAMPLE: a book written by Julieta Pinto was published by Editorial Costa Rica in the year 1976. The title of the book is "Cuentos de la Tierra". Editorial Costa Rica is located in San José.

Pinto, Julieta. *Cuentos de la Tierra*. San José: Editorial Costa Rica, 1976.

Or,

Pinto, Julieta. Cuentos de la Tierra. San José: Editorial Costa Rica, 1976.

Two authors

Books that are written by two authors are basically consigned in the same way, except that you include both names. According to the Modern Language Association rules, the first name is annotated as usual, but the second one is written with the first name ahead. The idea in this case is that bibliographic list are placed in alphabetical order according to the last name, which means that it makes no sense to write the second name in reverse. The book will be ordered according to the first author's last name any way.

Duncan, Quince and Carlos Meléndez. El Negro en Costa Rica. San José: Editorial Costa Rica, 1972.

Or:

Duncan, Quince and Carlos Meléndez. *El Negro en Costa Rica*. San José: Editorial Costa Rica, 1972

Notice that the second lines are indented. In other words if the citation is longer than one line, the second is indented. This makes the location of the book easier when searching in a list.

More than two authors

According to the Modern Language Association rules, the first name is annotated as usual, but the second and third is written with the first name ahead. If there are more than three, optionally, only the first name is consigned followed by the term "et al" (and others).

Let's take the case of a book written by Carlos Durán, Tencio Meléndez, Petronila Vargas y Onomatopeya Ragonés.

Durán, Carlos, et. al. *La mujer de frontera*. San José: Editorial Suave Luz, 1999.

Reeditions

In case the book has been published several times, the number of edition or reprinting should be consigned after the name of the book.

Meléndez, Carlos and Quince Duncan. *El Negro en Costa Rica*. 11th ed. San José: Editorial Costa Rica, 2005.

Institutional materials

If the material was published in the name of an institution, the name of the institution is used as author.

Costa Rica, Ministerio de Educación Pública, Dirección de Planeamiento y Desarrollo Educativo. Unidad de Administración Regional. <u>*Manual de Procedimientos para administrar las Escuelas de Verano*</u>. San José: Departamento de Publicaciones del MEP, 1980

The Writing Center, University of North Carolina. <u>Writing Business Letters</u>. USA: University of North Carolina at Chapel Hill, 2010.

Encyclopedias.

If Authors are indicated

Bowes, Antonio. "Las galaxias". Encyclopedia Golán. 1957-1958 ed.

If Authors are not indicated

"Spectral response for phosphate metabolism in germination lettuce seeds". *Encyclopedia of the Sciences*. Grolier 1984 ed.. V.9.

Ed. Stands for edition. V for volume.

Articles

An article from a printed magazine

Battes, Nolan. "Notes on alternative medicine". International Med Association Bulletin. Num. 138-139, 1987: pp. 4575-485.

An article from a newspaper:

Mendoza, Juan Luís. "No todo lo legal es moral" La República. (San José, Costa Rica), 20 de abril de 1991, p.12 col 2-3.

In this case "col" stands for column.

Graduate dissertation. (Thesis)

Osés Cordero, Guillermo Emilio. "Analysis of positivist ideas in "El Sitio de las Abras", of Fabián Dobles. Or:" In Search of the Lost Paradise". Dissertation to opt for the degree of Licenciatura in Literature and Language Sciences. School of Literature and Language Sciences: Universidad Nacional, 1976.

Online materials.

Journals:

Murillo, Álvaro. "Estrecho resultado electoral incide en selección de gabinete". La Nación Digital, (9.3.06) Online. 03.09.2006

If the information taken is a photo, image, an article or parts of it, you add the internet reference at the end of the material. You also add the word Online, the date and hour when you copied the material. The reason for this is that internet pages are subject to updates, and sometimes the material is totally retired.

EXAMPLE

Check this Illustration online

http://es.wikipedia.org/wiki/Ceremonia_Online 1/23/2010 6:25:21 AM

A sound recording

Molina, Alba. Flying on Fire. CD. AM International, 2006.

A movie

Caribe. Playwrite Ana Iztarú. Director Esteban Ramírez. Staring Jorge Perugorría, Cuca Escribano and Maya Zapata. Produce by Estaban Ramírez, 2004

A video recording

The Forgotten Root. Rebollar, Rafael, Director. Producer Trabuco S.C. México, 2001.

An Email

Jan, Fritz. "Women are hitting us hard". E-mail to Gigi Pérez, May 23, 2015.

A TV program

Elephants. NGO TV. U.S.A.: March 15, 2005.

A radio program

Hablando Claro. Ibarra, Vilma. Director. Radio Columbia. Costa Rica. December 6, 2009.

A work of art

Campos, Luis Enrique. La Partida de Gangán. Private collection of Quince Duncan, Santo Domingo de Heredia.

Picasso, Pablo. Guernica. Centro de Arte Reina Sofía, Madrid.

An interview

Durán, Enoé. "Genisis of the National University". Personal interview with Ladislao Gámez, Former Minister of Education. Heredia, Costa Rica. Abril 12, 2005.

An advertisement

Derma Wand. Advertisement. Chanel 7 San José. March 1º, 2009

A map or a Chart

Limon. Map. San José: Geographic Institute, 2001.

THEME 11 Sample Tesina

West College

Traditional Medicine in New Line Community
Use of Ginger.

Enos Duncanson
Undergraduate Research Report

Tutor Professor Reina Reyes

March 10, 2009

TABLE OF CONTENTS

Introduction

The present dissertation, argues that Afro Caribbean communities are in danger of losing many traditional knowledge that has been part of their lore in the field of health. These know-how's have been applied to the prevention and cure of diseases, be it alternatively or complementary.

This knowledge that has been orally transmitted is exposed to be appropriated by other sectors of the population, without recognition, and to fail to be the heritage of the Afro-descendant community. In general terms, these usages of plants are not known among the circles of practitioners of official medicine, and in any case, do not have enough prestige to gain the respect of the young people, who opt for a science divorced from their tradition and from some of the specific needs of the Black population.

In fact, there are four of the young people in New Line who are currently enrolled in studies in the field of medicine and nursing. We had the opportunity to talk with three of them, none of which showed any interest in the traditional knowledge of medicine.

The main idea of this dissertation is to contribute to the conservation of such knowledge that will be placed at the service of the new generations. The idea is not only to preserve as if they were parts of a museum of ancient artifacts, rather, it stems from the premise that the overwhelming majority of these skills are still in force. And, that at best, the paper will enhance the knowledge of natural remedies used in New Line, for the treatment, prevention and cure of some endemic and epidemic diseases, applicable in other parts of the country. So that the beneficiaries will be in first place the same community, New Line, and secondly, the entire national community that will benefit from these alternative treatments as a means to influence the health of a community that, at least in the rural areas, still sees in the natural medicine its first choice.

The proposed objectives were in general, to retrieve a body of ancient knowledge on natural health from a Caribbean population, New Line, documenting them scientifically, putting them at the service of the new generations. More specifically, it sought to identify a plant or medicinal herb commonly used in the afro-caribbean New Line community and analize it's use in this dissertation, properly documented from a scientific perspective of those herbs or plants.

The information on the traditional medicinal knowledge and beliefs of the people was obtained through 5 interviews with people who practice traditional medicine in the community.

The work, by its very nature, is descriptive, as its central goal is the description of the therapeutic practices based on the information gathered. The data source is the structured interviews sustained in extensive conversations with some of the therapists and to a lesser extent, the direct observation of the plants and the photographic documentation.

Ginger in New Line Community

As planned, a series of five interviews were carried out with therapists from the popular afro-caribbean community from New Line. The questionnaires were applied, and the information was supplemented in all cases with good conversation. In the study, we identified more than 20 plants that are used by these therapists. However, among all the plants the one with the largest presence was ginger.

Ginger is a perennial herb with an erect stem. It grows up to 90 cms. It's leaves has an elongated form and may extend up to 20 centimeters long. The flowers are grouped in green with yellow and dark violet spots.

This plant, whose scientific name is Zingiber officinale, belongs to the Zingiberaceae family, native to the tropical areas of Southeast Asia. The original name sringavera means "in the form of horn" in ancient Sanskrit language. It was incorporated into the Latin as zingiber and English as ginger. China and India are the main producers followed by the north of Australia and Hawaii. It is cultivated intensively in the Caribbean area and very sharply in the town of New Line. It is said that the Jamaican ginger is the best.

According to studies by Miranda (1980) and Mena (1994) cited by Rodriguez (2000: p.104), the leaves and stems contain "essential oil, alkaloids, flavonodes". In fact, the plant contains essential oil in abundance (0.5 to 3 %) zingerona, gingerol and shogaol and other substances. Precisely the gingerol, which is a yellow liquid, derives its spicy quality. The part of the plant used for curative purposes is the root (or rhizome). This grows horizontally, branched out in the soil and can grow to measure more than 1 meter.

It is used in a natural way, by cutting into pieces the fresh root, or scratching it or by grinding. It is also used in dehydrated form and powder.

MEDICINAL USE: The five informants consulted, praised the use of this plant.

Informant 1: He is a man of about 55 years who specializes in a massage system known in the area as "rubbing". He uses the ginger as an analgesic and an anti-inflammatory. He spells ginger water on a clean cloth, so that the substance completely soaks the cloth. Then, the cloth is tied over the sore part of the body. It is useful for joint pains, lumbago, sciatica, rheumatism.

Informant 2 is an older woman, who came to the area of New Line from Jamaica, when her parents immigrated. At that time, she said that she must have been about four years old. Her knowledge was inherited from her mother.

She also uses ginger as an analgesic and anti-inflammatory remedy. However, she uses it in infusions. She said that ginger is effective for rheumatic pains because it relieves pain and improves the mobility of the affected limb. She uses approximately one teaspoon of ginger in a cup of water, bringing to boiling point. She then, removes it from the heat and let it settle down and cool off. And then, it is ready to re-warm and drink.

Informant 3 is the person of the highest level of education of all informers. She even had formal studies in Chinese Herbology with a teacher. She argues that ginger is the best thing to prevent or treat cardiovascular disease and carries records of persons treated. She showed the records of 11 people to us, who had managed to reduce their levels of cholesterol dramatically and in short-terms.

She showed us an additional file belonging to a woman for whom the treatment did not work, but she believes that in reality the lady did not follow the indications. This informant also told us that ginger is a vasodilator. Also, she said that ginger can be used for head ailments such as migraine. The informant warned us that we had to be careful with ginger because in cases of stomach ulcer and fever, this plant is counter-indicated.

Informant 4, confirmed in more simple terms what was said by the informant 2 about the use of ginger in cases of headache, high cholesterol and heart disease. In all cases they use a piece of fresh root of approximately two centimeters and put it to simmer and boil.

Informants differ in realtion to how many times a day should the intake be. Informant 2 calculates the dose depending on the age and size of the person, while informant 4 does not have a fixed size but prescribes, he says, "as the spirit prompted". He emphasized that in fact all real healing is spiritual.

Informant 5, a lady of 60 years, who mentioned with much pride how they pondered ginger for its multiple uses. The list includes uses for stomach pain, fever, indigestion, vomiting, cough, flatulence, asthma, bronchitis, influenza, swelling of the throat, rheumatism. She prepares an infusion with three or four spieces of ginger root, depending on the thickness. Placing it in a "little" water, she brings it to boiling point. When the water begins to make bubbles she adds a few leaves of lemon grass and then leaves it on low-fire. In the case of affections of the throat, such as bronchitis, she adds two teaspoons of honey. The infusion should be warm. The lady said that it can also be applied in compresses to relieve bone pain.

There are accounts of the use of ginger for pregnancy nausea, and there is a single testimony of cancer cure. By the description she gave us, we could infer that it was a case of chemotherapy.

USE OF THE GINGER AS FOOD

It is interesting that the two female informants and informant 3 spoke about the uses of ginger in the kitchen. There are recipes for ginger bread which is sweet bread with ginger. There are also gingerbread biscuits. But the most common use in the kitchen, in the case of New Line is as a condiment. It is used for seasoning meat and fish. It is added to vegetables, rice and pasta. It is also used to prepare soups, jams, pickles, candy fruit and desserts based on this amazing plant

We also encountered the use of ginger in drinks. Very famous in New Line is ginger beer and ginger ale. We got the recipe for the "ale", which is in reality lemonade with ginger and sugar of panela. However, none of the respondents wanted to provide us with the recipe for the beer. In the end, we got it on the Internet and it seemed interesting, because it is a homemade product. However, it has the problem that in Costa Rica the production of alcohol is a monopoly of the State.

Ginger beer recepe:

- ✓ Cut up 6 large lemons and then remove the seeds
- ✓ Add 16 liters of boiling water
- ✓ Add 6 cups of sugar and 90 grams of crushed ginger.
- ✓ Let it boil for 15 minutes, and leave it to cool down.
- ✓ Once cool, add 2 or 3 cups of yeast diluted in water.
- ✓ Then, let it rest a day or two.

If you want to do it by a completely traditional method to give you the flavor of the beers of yesteryears, it is recommended that you do the recipe in a clay vase and cover it with a canvas. After it is strained put it in bottles, but be careful with filling it up to the tap since plugs can be expelled by pressure. You then keep it in a cool place for at least 3 months before serving.

Information retrieved from http://perso.wanadoo.es/e/piponet/Paginas/Elalquimista01.htm.

Conclusions.

As it has been presented all through the present paper, there is an ancestral knowledge in New Line community that is worth saving. Some of it, as in the case of ginger, can be of great utility for both traditional medicine and for culinary uses, but also in the manufacture of healthy drinks. This accumulation of asymmetrical ancestral knowledge into the community of New Line has not been validated lately to a satisfactory level.

We acknowledge that there are some efforts to perform scientific studies on traditional medicine. Good examples are the studies by Rosita Arvigo and Michael Balick (1993); Hernan Rodriguez (2000) and the Caribbean Pharmacopoeia Tramil (2005). These are examples of efforts in that direction.

This research study was able to document some of this knowledge. This dissertation presents the case of one plant, for reasons of space and time, but the author's intention is to continue the study, increasing the sample of the 20 plants documented, to at least 60 with the intention to publish it in a small book and return the knowledge to the community.

References.

Tramil. Farmacopea Vegetal Caribeña. 2da ed. República Dominicana: Editorial universitaria UNANA.León, 2005.

Rodriguez Navas, Hernán. Utilidad de las plantas medicinales. San José: EUNA, 2000.

Arvigo, Rosita y Michael Balick. Rainforest remedies. USA: Lotus, 1993.

Duncanson, Enos. "Uso de las plantas medicinales en New Line del Caribe". Entrevista Informante 1, Terapeuta Popular. New Line: marzo 25, 2005.

Duncanson, Enos. "Uso de las plantas medicinales en New Line del Caribe". Entrevista Informante 2, Terapeuta Popular. New Line: marzo 26, 2005.

Duncanson, Enos. "Uso de las plantas medicinales en New Line del Caribe". Entrevista Informante 3, Terapeuta Popular. New Line: abril 3, 2005.

Duncanson, Enos. "Uso de las plantas medicinales en New Line del Caribe". Entrevista Informante 4, Terapeuta Popular. New Line: abril 3, 2005.

Duncanson, Enos. "Uso de las plantas medicinales en New Line del Caribe". Entrevista Informante 5, Terapeuta Popular. New Line: abril 3, 2005.

THEME 12 Defense of Your Tesina

You will be required to make two final presentations. The first will be a preliminary presentation to School authorities. They will approve your work with specific recommendations for your public defense. You will then proceed to incorporate suggestions and make the necessary changes, and present your final written "tesina" to your advisor for grading.

Illustration 11: **Remember, when presenting your tesina, you are the expert.**

The School Principal will set up a date for public defense.

Protocol
To follow protocol is vital to the speaker.

✓ Opening
▪ Greet the members of the main table by names and positions. Remember saluting the person in the highest position first.
▪ Address the Director by name
▪ Address school authorities (Dear Teacher)

- Address Visitors
- Address fellow students

Dear Mr/Ms Boxter, School Director. Dear Professors. My Best regards to visitors, thank you for being here. Fellow students…

✓ Enunciate your topic very clearly.

You want your audience to be aware of the content of your paper from the very beginning. Open with an attention grabbing sentence or idea. A good way is to use your paper title or a descriptive statement but don't make it too long.

You are interested in capturing and retaining the interest of the listeners. You may use your central idea, your thesis. The thesis of your report is aimed at creating an impact or to cause controversy. After presenting the point that you want to make, you may then develop supporting ideas during the rest of your presentations.

A speech can be delivered in different "emotional tones". You may speak assertively, in a confrontation mood in relation to the audience. In that case you may be positively challenging the audience, or being hostile or rude. The option to this is to speak in an insecure fearful tone. A third possibility is to be very apathetic.

It is better to use a high tone. Speak assertively. Remember, you did the research, you are the expert.

✓ Mention a few sources consulted — the most important.

You, of course want the audience to know that you are acquainted with the content of the field. But you do not have the time to mention all sources used in collecting your data. Furthermore, it can be boring. So limit yourself to mention two or three.

✓ Move on to the core.

Introduce a generic or central idea that justifies the whole speech. By central idea we must understand the essential message to be conveyed.

The speaker presents his or her thesis gradually as the speech develops. He or she recurs to awe, humor, data, reflexive thought, and persuasiveness to mobilize the audience.

During this portion you will be denying something or proposing something. That is, the demonstration or confirmation of the thesis, with data, convincing arguments and examples. You will be presenting the product of experimentation, the results of analysis and the theoretical cognitions. Present your arguments orderly, with logic. During the body of the speech, you are expected to use articulate and convincing arguments. Use definitions, comparisons, cause-effect sequences, give examples and be logical.

✓ Keep focus on your subject. Describe whatever process might be evolved, but be always coherent in relation to your objectives, or whatever your thesis statement may be.

✓ Present your conclusions and recommendations.

You recall the original thesis and give a synthesis of the matter, emphasizing that you have reached a solid standing on the matter. You make a synthesis of the main idea, showing how your problem was solved, or your thesis statement sustained.

Conclude, if pertaining, with recommendations about how to apply the result of your work or give some idea about possible future research that could be made to follow-up on the subject.

✓ Closing

Thank your advisor for his support and thank the audience for their attention.

✓ Offer to take a few questions on the matter.

Be prepared to answer whatever questions posed with courtesy. Avoid entering into a reactive conflict with the audience. You must pre-suppose that every question is made in good will.

✓ Avoid aggressiveness.

To get angry when you are confronted may be seen as a lousy way to hide ignorance. If you do not have an answer, say so in a polite calm way. For example, "I did not find an answer to that question during my research"; or, "Your observation is interesting, but I did not look over the matter from that point of view". There might be someone in the audience that does not like your conclusions or recommendations. That's fine. Just avoid boring and useless confrontations.

✓ Smile. Always end on a high tone.

INFORMATION FOR EXPERTS

You are now very close to completing this course. The information that follows is for experts. If you are one, go ahead. Read, study and complete this book. If you don't feel like an expert, well, go ahead. At the end of this final section, you may well become one.

A Panel Presentation

Illustration 12: **A panel presentation**

A research paper presented as part of a panel, in general terms, is one possible way to give account of a study. It is delivered in two parts: a written essay and an oral presentation.

Papers are normally called for. That is, an institution organizes a panel on one or more related subjects, and sends out a call for papers. Researches interested in the theme, respond offering a paper on any of the topics. They have to submit a proposal containing two elements: a title for the paper and an abstract or summary of one a page, in which he or she enunciates the objectives and the central ideas that the paper will contain.

The organizing committee revises the abstract and accepts or rejects the proposal. If it is approved, a written consent is forwarded to the proposer.

Once approved, the panelist presents the written version, which must be four to six pages double spaced. This is sent in advance to the organizing committee, which, if possible, reproduces in printed form or in a CD copies for all attendants, or puts the papers on line so that each person can download and read the papers before the event.

Once in the event, and according to the program, the panelist makes an oral presentation, which should be a summary of the paper. Reading is not recommended, since the written form of communication is not exactly the same as an oral presentation.

The time assigned normally ranges between 15 and 20 minutes. Panelists must keep in the time framework, since when there time is over the person presiding the table, will interrupt the speaker, and the exposition will not be completed.

It is always preferable to prepare a good summary, a synthesis with the main points. In any case anyone interested will already have read the paper or will be able to do so when it is published.

Writing Essays

An essay is a relatively short composition based on a single subject. In writing an essay, the author presents his personal view on the subject.

Essays can be based on the description of a specific scene. To describe is to give an account of a picture or scene using words.

Describing Scenes

What elements are useful to bear in mind when writing a description?

Space. Distance: near, close, far.

Is the environment seems harmonious, peaceful, hostile, menacing or neutral.

Describe objects that you observe. Take into account size, weight, forms, colors, tactile sensation (smooth, rough, cold, warm, etc.).

Describe living things, their forms, attitudes, movements.

You may establish and describe relations between living things and unanimated objects.

Present psychological factors if necessary. Is the person, animal or whatever described deeply rooted in the environment or rather marginal?

You may want to analyze the ecological relations. Are they positive, negative, conflictive?

You may also want to imagine and comment on the causes and consequences involved in whatever situation you are describing.

A good way to get started when writing a descriptive essay is to make a list of what you see, hear, feel, smell, and taste. A list of colors, forms, sizes, odors—all these details may contribute to a sentence or paragraph.

STEPS LEADING TO A SUCCESFUL ESSAY

Topics of course, could be assigned by the teacher. In this case, you still have certain degree of liberty to be creative. You must limit your subject, and give it an approach that might be as interesting as you can get. Make sure you understand what is expected: a very general overview or a specific analysis. Can you analyze the subject freely, or are you required to use a given procedure? If you are free to choose to topic then make sure you pick a topic that is of interest to you.

You must then establish your purpose. What do you want to convey to the potential reader?

Don't forget to limit your topic. It should not be too wide or narrow. For example, "Coffee in Costa Rica" would force you to write a very long essay on the many aspects related—growth, industrialization, marketing, exportation, consumption… Definitely that is too wide for an essay. But "Coffee plantations in Costa Rican Highlands" might be easier to cover.

Write an outline. It will be tentative at this early stage, since when writing you may want to include or eliminate parts of it. No problem: be free to change your outline if necessary, but make a tentative one to keep yourself on track. The idea is to avoid wandering from one idea to another, since doing so will take you nowhere.

An outline is made up of main ideas and supporting ideas. For example:

Two types of coffee produced in C.R. Highlands

Arabica, and canephor robusta

Arabica from Abyssinia (Ethiopia)

Grows on mountains and plateau in altitudes ranging from 700 to 2000 meters.

Grows in subtropical zone

Mild taste

Canephor Robusta from Zaire

Can grow in jungle areas

Fast growing

Stronger taste

Essays are made up of three parts: introduction, body and conclusions.

You must write your body first. In this section you should explain, describe, and argue. Use each point of your outline to write a paragraph. In the example above, "Two types of coffee produced in C.R. Highlands" would be the main idea of the section. Numbers 1, 2, 3, are main ideas for paragraphs, while a, b and c are supporting ideas corresponding to each paragraph.

Finally, write the introductory and conclusive paragraph. The function of the introduction is to attract the reader's attention and give an idea of the essay's content and focus. The conclusion points to the main idea of the whole text you may describe your feelings about the subject, or a final thought that you would like to share with the reader.

TRY OUT YOUR HAND…

Write a short essay on any of the following scenes.

Illustration 13: **Look at this scene. Imagine what is going on.**

Narration

> To narrate is to describe action. In a narration, there is a narrator telling a story to a receptor, directly as it in the case of a newspaper article or indirectly in the case of a work of fiction. Things are happening, moving from an initial situation, progressing toward a climax and ending.

Read the following sample story. Make sure you indentify the inicial situation of the story, the progression and the climax and ending.

If you choose to write a narrative, remember that these are the basic parts of any narrative.

Antofagasta

By Quince Duncan

Translated by Alan Garfinkel

When I crossed the border into Chile and the immigration officer welcomed me with a "You're going to have a great time because in Chile we love Blacks," I prepared myself for war.

It's the same way everywhere, I told myself. I am always suspicious of people who constantly declare their love of Blacks because it's difficult to believe a guy who abstractly loves Blacks or Whites or Chinese. One could love one Black person, but all of them?

I did not sense any evidence of racism on the bus. Moreover, there was no seat available which is why the driver offered to let me sit on a board that he would place between the seats. I accepted, at least to get to Antofagasta from which it would be easy to get transportation to Santiago. It was hard traveling through half of northern Chile sitting on a board, but it was my only choice.

A lady showed me sympathy and said that if her daughter would ride in my lap, I could have her seat.

From that moment on I began the slow but sure process of seduction until, some forty minutes later, the little girl was asleep in my lap.

We arrived a little after dawn. I went out to walk through the streets of Antofagasta to breathe the air and get to know some of the city.

I was enjoying my walk, fascinated by the city when I heard the yell of a girl.

"Mommy, come see!!! There's a Black man coming. There's a Black man!"

Fortunately, I was prepared for war.

I had about 25 paces during which to search my memory for the right recipe for a reply. I had developed several to deal with this kind of situation. It could be, for example, "don't settle for just seeing me. Why don't you come touch me"? ...or maybe, cruder yet, like, "Gee, those Chileans sure are dumb brutes."... Or hasn't your daughter ever seen a Black man? The idea was to run through my repertory and, fortunately I still had about 22 paces to decide.

Twenty-one paces to come out of the situation elegantly.

I breathed deeply. I think that at 19 paces, my hands began to sweat. It's just not the same confronting racism in one's own country, as dealing with that phenomenon in the middle of Latin America's Southern Cone region.

But it was clear that I was right... really right. That's just what it was: I knew. It's a question of experience. It was obvious that from the moment that that immigration officer told me that I was going to have a good time in Chile, I just knew it. It's the same all over the world.

Nine paces.

By now the mother summoned was on the sidewalk. Next to her the girl who chanted the news and two other women. I observed the mother well and I saw her taking position. Without doubt, she wanted to be close to me; I imagined the laughter, the teasing that would be drawn on her face; and maybe I was going to want to attack her without being able to do so. First, because she was a woman and second, because in my house, I was always taught never to respond to violence with more violence.

Five paces.

I was definitely in the lion's mouth.

Saliva was building up in my throat. A forced smile on my face. One must be well mannered, very well mannered. It was necessary to show these people what courtesy and culture really are. It was necessary to show them a well mannered Black man, who knows how to defend himself without dodging, who does not let the thing go, but does not react in a manner that would validate the stereotype.

Two paces. The older woman in front of me. Directly in front of me, blocking my way. I couldn't walk out into the street. That was not manly. I must not leave these Chileans with the impression that Blacks were brutish fools. So, in my last seconds I got to breathing heavily and raised my head to sustain her glance which was already searching for mine.

The woman stood in the middle of the sidewalk directly in front of me and had her say.

"You are so handsome!"

I don't know where I found the cool and calm I needed in order to give the only possible reply.

"Thanks."

And I had a great time in Chile.

Illustration 14: Write a story about this police

A Humoristic Text

If you were a child during the 60s and 70s, or even during the first part of the 80s, how did you manage to survive?

Children did not have to use seat belts or air bags in cars… Riding in the back of a pickup truck was a special treat that we still remember. Our cots were painted with bright colors of lead-based paint. There were no insurance for children against bottles of medicine, cabinets, and doors.

We drank water from the garden hose and not from a bottle. We spent hours and hours building carts form scrap. Whe rode our bikes without helmets or breaks, and rushed down hilly streets without even thinking about brakes. After several clashes with the bushes we learned to solve the problem. Yes, we fought with bushes, not with cars! We went out to play with the only condition to return home before nightfall.

School lasted until noon, we arrived home for lunch. We had no cellphones… no smartphones so nobody could trak us down. We broke a bone here and there, lost a tooth, but there was never a legal demand for those accidents. Nobody was to blame but ourselves. We ate pretzels, bread and butter, drank drinks with sugar and never had overweight because we were always outside playing … We shared a drink between four … drinking from the same bottle and no one died. We had no PlayStations, Nintendo 64, X boxes, video games, 99 channels of cable TV, video recorders, theater, surround sound, computers, chat rooms on the Internet …

But we had friends. We went out. We jumped on the bike or walked to the house of a friend. We talked about the marble game… or simply went out to play.

There, outside, in the cruel world, without a guardian! How did we survive? We had games with sticks and tennis balls, and we just formed a team to play a game.

At school some flunked. But it did not lead them to trauma. Some students were not as bright as others and when they flunked they repeated. No one had to go to the psychologist, psychopedagogist, nobody had dyslexia. They simply repeated and had a second chance.

We had freedom, failure, success, responsibilities … and learned how to handle them.

The younger generations may say that our lives were boring. But, were we a happy lot!

Adapted from the INTERNET. Author Anonymous.

Poetic Prose

And, Paris…

Because Paris captives and releases with its goblins and ghosts beside whom one walks to the edge of its legendary river and step in the shadows of people long gone; across the bridges and the parks and the ancient buildings, and impringe oneself in the ancient art galaries surviving in spite of the transnational corporations alongside the eternal temples and cathedrals that humankind cherish; because as we have been well taught by our poets, mistery is lovely, and then the old cafes with their goblins and fraternal ghosts that come back to life each time we shout or scream freedom. Freedom, and you have survived in the memories and experiences immortalised by the authors we have read and the fictional world that were created and the reality and the imaginary "overlays" there in perfect concurrency and the amount of time spent on each street that feeds on what was said by philosophers and of what they had proposed in their treaties and the echoes of the painters creating in us the collective memory and the voices that sing from their batons and the word of all those who opened the door to our full understanding that Paris is history and passion and dream and is black and is white and is gray and is the color. Paris is time and it is also the very vision of time and the perception of what was and what is; what has to be and all floating in the air and the taste and the smell of the flowers and the freshness of a city where nothing happens and everything happens and always passes and never goes and that puts nostalgia in the eyes of the oldest humanity and hope in the chest of the nascent humanity because Paris captive us and releases and...

EXAMPLE OF A FORMAL LECTURE

ACTIVITY:
While reading, identify the listed parts of this speech. Use paragraph numbers.

Introducction. Starts _____Ends_____
Descriptive argument Starts _____Ends_____
Use of definition Starts _____Ends_____
Listing Starts _____Ends_____
Contrast Starts _____Ends_____
Body of speech Starts _____Ends_____
Justification of speech (subject) Starts _____Ends_____
Transition word. At paragraph _____
Use of examples Starts _____Ends_____
Conclusions Starts _____Ends_____

I.O.I. CONGRESS
THE GREATER CARIBBEAN:
NATURE AND CULTURE AS DYNAMICAL CONCEPTS

1. Mr. President, conference members:
2. It is a Great honor for me to concur before this distinguished audience, in order to share some ideas about culture with you. My words are intended above all to be an invitation to reflection.
3. I will begin by defining the cultural area object of this dissertation, and then go on to justify culture as a important subject in an event like this, relating to the sea and peace.
4. We will then discuss the culture of the Greater Caribbean, in order to point out a couple of cultural values I esteem relevant to this forum. In fact the focus that we are going to give to this presentation is that the Greater Caribbean is more than a sea.
5. And finally, I have adventured to relate sea, peace and the Greater Caribbean under the focus of ethics, hoping to challenge you as a group to go beyond formulas because I know as well as you does that when dealing with Human culture recipes won't do.
6. Definition of the term
7. Cultural area:
8. Considered from the cultural point of view, the Greater Caribbean is an area that extends from New Orleans in the North, to the Guayanas in the South of the Continent, incorporating on the way Veracruz, the Atlantic Costa of Central America, the Atlantic Coast of the northern part of South America, the Islands of the Caribbean and extending to embrace the entire Belize and most of the Isthmus of Panama.
9. One can describe the Greater Caribbean as being a zone with a vast cultural diversity, but at the same time, because of its traditional links with colonial powers and the decisive presence of the African culture, the Greater Caribbean has been able to forge certain characteristics that distinguish it as a cultural entity with unique identity.
10. Importance of studying culture
11. So what is the importance of the studying the culture of the Greater Caribbean in a forum like this? After all, the conference has been summoned in order to analyze the issue of the sea.
12. I believe that the very title of the conference explains that importance. PACEM IN MARIBUS. And peace is a human concept.

It is a product of culture. After all, nature was not at war. Nature acts on the principle of survival and proceeds in accordance to protect itself as a system. Survival is a natural law blindly observed by nature. SURVIVE. So then, if there is a distortion in the process of construction, deconstruction and natural reconstruction, it has been introduced by the human being.

13. This is because human beings are not compelled by blind obedience. It is rather a critical and self interested type of obedience, not always centered on the survival of life as such, but on the survival of a specific group. A reductionist position is adopted: suddenly there is a company, or government, or organization, and even individuals that prefix their own survival to that of nature itself. And that is the origin of war. That is why we lack peace, on earth and sea.

14. Nevertheless, there is a curious fact. Humanity continues to be concerned about its own "destruction" or transformation into any inferior state, different from the human condition. Humanity continues to be concerned over any possible loss of its condition as beings conscious of being conscious. And while nature solves its own equation the human being faces two sides of a coin: on the one hand he is aware of having created his own problem and on the other hand, he knows that to find or not to find a way out defines nothing less than his survival as a species.

15. Sometimes scientists and politicians join hands. Occasionally for the better. Now and again for the worst. Scientist spent much of their time locked in their laboratories, producing knowledge or going to the fields to checkout their hypothesis. The politician walks the streets promising and sometimes promoting development. The scientist may say that the problem in fact is not his and that social problems correspond to social sciences and to politics. But the social sciences have enormous difficulties in advancing, because as soon as they have hardly set up a theory that works, the human being, object of study decides to demolish the existent relationships and build another. And they all fail because ideology blinds them. I refer to the ideology of those who have an ideology. And I also refer to the ideology of those who say they don't have an ideology.

16. What is very clear is the fact that no science can advance, without considering culture. Transfusion technology is useless in a community where it is taboo to have the blood of another person.

17. Culture matters because it is as a result of culture that war is declared. And it is only by means of a change in culture that we will achieve peace.

18. Sometimes the specialists, the scientists, and especially the politicians commit very serious hostile acts against humanity without realizing it. They exclude cultural values from their decisions, and recommendation processes. Ancestral convictions, cultural elements and systems, have an enormous specific weight on the mind of the scientist who is reputed as more objective. But civil society is not illustrated and is more inclined to handling matters intuitively rather than to do so in compliance with the rigor of scientific discipline.

19. In order to illustrate the importance of considering the cultural processes in all our decisions and recommendations, allow me to bring up two interesting examples that I have taken from my own experience, as part of a team integrated by the World Council of Churches some years ago, to express solidarity to the Aborigines of Australia.

20. In interviews with local authorities of colonial mentality, entrusted of the reservations, they expressed to us their assessments on the Aboriginal population. According to those points of view, the Australian natives were destined to disappear because they were unable to be integrated into the Western Civilization. And they gave several examples in order to sustain their point of view. Among the examples that gave us, I have chosen two to share them with you, because as we traveled through that vast and beautiful Continent we had the opportunity to hear the other version.

21. Case of the Nurses

22. By means of one of their programs guided to incorporate the Aborigines to the "benefits of progress" the Australian Government had granted scholarships and formed a group of nurses to assist in their community. When graduated, the nurses began to serve their people efficiently, but with a bias: they would not attend to all sectors of the population. In vain the officials tried to change that situation. But there seemed to be no way to convince them to do so.

23. Of course, in the eyes of the racists' authorities of the provincial governments this was a monumental absurdity and a demonstration of the inability of the Aborigines to assimilate progress, but there

was a simple and logical explanation if one takes the viewpoint of the local culture.

24. During one of our sessions with the aborigines, one of our "groundings" as goes the typical Aborigine expression for thinking in community, we discovered that the government had made a huge error. The selection system, rigorous beyond doubt was based on scholarly skills. This system had determined the selection and training of women of the same generation. In that culture this was a very serious mistake, since it is taboo for a person to see the nakedness of his/her mothers, that is to say, the nakedness of the women generationally contemporary to their mother. So having chosen all of the nurses from the same generation, none could assist to the excluded sector, for this would have been a dangerous violation of the cultural convictions — a great sin.

25. All of this could have been avoided if, previous to selection of the trainees, some of the scientists or politicians had sat down with the community "in grounding." But arrogance, prejudice and self-sufficiency excluded any attempt to listen to the point of view of the local community which certainly was considered "primitive".

26. Case of the Houses

27. The second case that we succeeded to clarify in our "groundings" with the Aborigines is that of the houses. Indeed, it was a matter of much surprise that, after the Government invested thousands of Australian dollars in the construction of houses for the Aborigines, the community used them as warehouses and continued sleeping on the outside, near the earth.

28. But once you saw the houses and heard the community you could easily understand. These houses would have been great for Germans, Scots or Irishmen. To begin with, they were not in the correct position. The Aborigines of that ethnic group sleep in certain position, in accordance with the magnetic poles of the Earth. The houses were not placed properly according to their culture, and they therefore preferred to use them as warehouses. Also, to sleep in them was to estrange themselves from Mother Earth and she, in the Australian cosmology, nurtures the human being during his hours of rest.

29. Again we here see how the lack of a proper "grounding", prevented a proper "setting in common", and lead to a "setting in failure."

30. And the Australian scientists and politicians justified their own failure committing a new hostile act: they accuse the victim of being the cause of his own plight, and so liberating themselves from any responsibility.

31. Definitively, culture is the base of everything human. War and peace. The death of the species or their survival. For that reason it is important to meditate on culture in the context of this conference.

32. Ethics for survival

33. Well. This Conference is about building peace in the ocean about peace in the Greater Caribbean. Moreover, this should be an occasion to work for peace in general.

34. The North American thinker and educator L. Ronald Hubbard, the founder of the Dianetics sustains that the whole universe responds to a single law: survive.

35. As for the human being, there are eight ways in which this universal law tends to be followed. There are eight basic impulses that Mr. Hubbard called dynamics. The dynamics of existence.

36. The first dynamic, the first impulse is to survive as an individual being. The human being tries to live the longest possible time in the best living conditions that he can achieve. These conditions are not necessarily the accumulation of material wealth, but rather the achievement of personal goals that may or may not include material wealth. It is necessary when working for peace with the ocean to take into account that some people prefix their own personal survival, to that of the common interest.

37. The second dynamic refers to the relationships of sex and paternity-maternity. As human beings we strive to survival by means of our descendants. A compatible couple with such an aspiration tries to ensure continuity by means of their offspring. There is an interior impulse to guarantee that there will always be children. This is a very good reason to work for peace with nature. Damaging the sea is detrimental to our survival as a species.

38. But also the human being endeavors to survive as a group and ties his own personal realization to some type of group, be it an organization, company, movement, church, union, sport club. In all cultural formations high regard is given to the continuity of the group and the validity of the individual as a member of one or another group. This is the third dynamic. The third dynamic is one of the strongest barriers in relation to peace and the sea.

Social relations are conflictive, with one group striving to impose its view on the other, or as in the case of the Australians, simply not taking the other's view into account. How do we convey scientific findings in relation to the urge to protect and preserve the sea in such a way, that we convince multiple sectors of our third dynamic?

39. On the other hand, the existence of groups targeting such issues as human rights, nuclear threat, peace and eradication of illnesses and hunger in the world, give testimony to the fourth dynamics: the impulse toward the survival of the human species. Indeed, we all know that our destination on this Planet is bound to that of the whole human species. How can we enhance the capacity of those groups in there crusade for survival?

40. I believe that a group like this is a clear manifestation fifth dynamic: the survival of life itself. You are concerned with the flora and fauna of the seas. You are working to create awareness that the very survival of our species depends on the preservation of biodiversity. And you are also working with the sixth dynamic: the survival of the physical world represented by the acronyms: MEST, that is, MATTER, ENERGY, SPACE & TIME.

41. You are aware of the necessity to ensure that matter, energy, space and time lasts, because these are in fact our anchor points in this universe.

42. But mind you. You face human culture. The spiritual element, the seventh dynamic. The examples we used to illustrate the importance of culture should be a beacon for all of us. Human beings do not obey the law of survival blindly. Human beings do not adapt themselves to nature—they try adapting nature to themselves. There culture is important. Whether they believe in an eighth dynamic -God, the fact is that Human beings are endowed with dignity and are conscious of being conscious.

43. Toward an integrated ethical solution

44. As we have seen, Mr. Hubbard's survival theory proves very useful when building a set of criteria as we face the issue of peace in the seas, in the context of the Greater Caribbean. First, when confronting the challenge of peace in the seas, in the deliberations and in the decision making processes, it is essential to consider the human being in his/her individual dimension. Each person counts. Each person as an individual, beyond the boundaries of his/her particular group is entitled to be part of the solution. Man

or woman, girl or boy, a solution of peace for the seas should include the well-being of each person.

45. Second, true peace for the Greater Caribbean will have to consider the natural drive common to all people to perpetuate themselves by means of their descendants. Peace in the oceans means better conditions of health and food. A solution that leaves the children at bay starving to death is not a solution. Only by means of saving the children can we survive.

46. Peace in the oceans must consider that the Caribbean people and cultures have a natural right to survive as a cultural group, that have come a long way over the centuries, being created and creating itself from diversity, building common features that make that culture unique. In our efforts for peace we could learn a lot from the tolerance of the people of the Greater Caribbean. But a real peace in the relationships of the man with the sea the world over, should never omit the fact that the battle for peace in the Caribbean, the drive for construction and reconstruction is a battle for humanity. It is a struggle that benefits all of humanity. It is a fight in which we should all take part.

47. Equally important is it to emphasize, that the conservation of the ecological systems of the Greater Caribbean should be perceived in the context of the conservation of the ecosystems of the world.

48. Peace for the Greater Caribbean includes the conservation of physical world. MEST, if we are truly heading for a sustainable development and also for aesthetic delight becomes a vital part of our struggle.

49. Yes, peace is fundamentally an ethical principle. Peace in the oceans should take into account the dignity and the spiritual integrity of the human being including of course the dignity and spirituality of the Caribbean people.

50. And peace, if we are really heading for peace, should incorporate the world view of the Caribbean culture, respecting their deep universal convictions.

51. PACEM IN MARIBUS, INDEED.

52. It is an ethically correct proposal, because it is a matter of survival. And in the final battle for the planet, we are going to achieve our goals of survival if we consider the eight dynamics. Because experience has proven that it is not true that in the field of nature the strongest always survive. Definitively what is true is that the most capable are the strongest.

53. Looking at our surroundings we find abundant evidence that survival is the result of the effort of a group. So the survival of the greater Caribbean is directly related to the effort of the group. Peace in the seas has to do with our survival. His. Mine. Yours. The survival of our children. The survival of our neighbors. The survival of the other species. The survival of the physical world as we know it. The survival of the world for the countless future generations whose option of being born depends on each single one of our decisions. Yesterday are memories. Tomorrow is the reign of dreams, the mental field of postulates. Today is the reality that we share. But we build tomorrow from today. Pacem in maribus, should be the prelude to pacem in terra. And it will be so if your deliberations and decisions are led by ethical guidelines like the one I have shared with you. Faced as we all are with the dilemma of the reconstruction of the greater Caribbean, in face of the necessity to build peace in the seas, the all embracing ethical principle is to: seek that which produces the greatest good in the largest number of the eight dynamics.

End note:

Wow! You have made it to the end of the Learning to Learn Series. You are now prepared to present your undergraduate project.

In the future, research can become much more demanding. But you are in possetion of the basic characteristics the field.

The investigative attitude promoted during these courses, will be of use not only as an academic resort, but throughout your life.

Apply these techniques to all your activities. Set up objectives for your life as you go along, choose an adequate method and its corresponding procedures to solve problems and to obtain whatever your expected result might be; collect information in an orderly way and finally, present results in the best possible way—such should be your profile graduating out of the system.

Keep on the track.

REFERENCES

Aguilar, Marianela and Bogantes, Antonieta (1998). Manual para la Investigación de Campo. San José: Sistema Educativo Saint Clare.

American Psychological Association. Publication Manual (1994). 4ta. Ed. Washington: APA.

Ander-Egg, Ezequiel (1981). Introducción a las Técnicas de Investigación Social. 3a. edición. Panamá: Editorial Humanitas, S.A.

Asti, Armando (1973). Metodología de la Investigación. Buenos Aires: Kapelusz.

Bailey, Thomas and Eicher, Theo (1994). In, "Education, Technological Change and Economic Growth". Washington: Interamer/POEA, pp 103-120

Bedensky, León (1994). "Economía regional en la era de la globalización". In, Revista Comercio Exterior", Vol.44 (11).

Bonstingl, John Jay (1991). Introducction to the Social Sciences. New Jersey: Prentice Hall.

Carnoy, Martin (1992). "Education and the State: From Adam Smith to Perestroika". In, Emergent Issues in Education. Robert F, Arnove; Altbach, Philip; Gail, G.; Kelly, P. Editors. New York: State University of New York Press, pp.143-159

Castillejo, J.L. and Colom, A.J. (1987). Pedagogía Sistémica. Barcelona: Ceac.

CEPAL/UNESCO (1992). Educación y conocimiento: eje de la transformación productiva con equidad. Santiago de Chile: CEPAL.

Chen, Hilda (1980). "Para qué tipo de sociedad formamos?." Costa Rica: U.C.R.

Corzo, J.M (1973). Técnicas de Trabajo Intelectual. España: Ediciones Anaya.

Delors, Jacques et al (1996). La Educación Encierra un Tesoro. Madrid: Santillana/Ediciones Unesco.

Díaz Márquez, Luis (1997). Introducción a los estudios literarios. Puerto Rico: Editorial Plaza Mayor.

Duncan, Quince (1992) La Gran Aventura de Investigar. Heredia.

Duncan, Quince (1994) Pedagogía Sistémica Aplicada. San José.

Duncan, Quince; Howlett Leonor; Jiménez, Rosa María and Quirós, Nury (1986). Guía para la Investigación. San José: Editorial Nueva Década.

Duverger, Maurice (1962). Métodos de las Ciencias Sociales. Barcelona: Ediciones Ariel.

Fernández, Rodrigo (2004) Cómo Hablar en Público. Buenos Aires: Longseller.

Galván Escobedo, José (1979). Proceso Administrativo. San José: Editorial Universidad Estatal a Distancia.

García Canclini, Nestor (1995). Consumidores y ciudadanos. Conflictos multiculturales de la globalización. México: Grijalbo.

García Canclini, Nestor 1979). La Producción Simbólica. México: Siglo XXI.

Gardner, Howard (1983; 1993) Frames of Mind: The theory of multiple intelligences, New York: Basic Books.

Gardner, Howard (1993). La mente no escolarizada. Barcelona: Paidós.

Gibaldi, Joseph (1995) MLA Handbook for Writers of Research Papers. 6th. ed. New York: MLA.

Goleman, Daniel (1995). Emotional Intlligence. New York: Bantam Books.

Goleman, Daniel (2006). Inteligencia Social. Barcelona: Kairós.

Gómez Barrantes, M. (2005). Elementos de estadística descriptiva, 3ª edición. EUNED, San José, Costa Rica.

González Dobles, Jaime (1986) El Proceso Investigativo. San José: Alma Mater.

Goode, William; Hatt, Paul (1979). Métodos de la Investigación Social. Mexico: Editorial Trillas.

Gortari (De), Eli (1970). El Método Dialéctico. Mexico: Editorial Grijalbo, S.A.

Hernández Sampieri, R. et al. (1998). Metodología de la investigación, 2ª edición. McGraw-Hill, México D.F. México.

Hubbard, Ronald (1993). Manual Básico de Estudio. Los Angeles: Bridge Publications Inc.

Hubbard. L:.Ronald (1988). Autoanálisis. España: New Era Publications España, S.A.

Hurtado de Barrera, Jacqueline (2000). Metodología de la Investigación Holística. Caracas: SYPAL/IUTC.

Inter-Regional Center for Curriculum and Material Development (1983). Guidelines for Bi-National School Planning. Alabama U.S.A.

Jones, Beau Fly et. Al (1987). Estrategias para enseñar a aprender. Miguel Wald, translator. Buenos Aires: Aique Grupo Editor.

Karls, John B and Szymanski, Ronald (1995) TheWriter's Handbook. 2nd Ed. USA, Illinois: National Texbook Company.

Kientz, Albert (1976). Para Analizar los Mass Media. 2da. Ed. Valencia: Fernando Torres, Editor.

Kolb, David and Fry, R (1975). Toward an applied theory of experiential learning. In C. Cooper (ed.) Theories of Group Process, London: John Wiley,

Kubis, Pat and Howland, Bob (1990). The Complete Guide to Writing Fiction and Non Fiction. 2da. Ed. New Jersey: Prentice Hall.

Lawrence, Mary S (1976). Writing as a Thinking Process. 4ta. Ed. Michigan: University of Michigan Press.

Leñero, Vicente and Marín, Carlos (1986). Manual de Periodismo. México, Editorial Grijalbo.

León Mejía, Alma B(2004). Estrategias para el Desarrollo de la Comunicación Personal. México: Editorial Limusa.

León Villalobos, Edwin (, 1992). "El papel de la educación en tiempos de cambio". In, Horizontes. No. 2. San José: CENECOOP R.L, pp 41-47

Lesourne, Jacques (1988). Educación e Société. Les Defis de L'an 2000. París: Edition La Decouvert,. pp. 103-203.

Litton, Gaston (1971). La Informacion de la Biblioteca Moderna. Argentina: Centro Regional de Ayuda Tecnica.

Malavassi Rojas, Eduardo; Saborío Elizondo, Lidieth; Bustos Mora, Giselle (2005). Programa nacional de ferias de ciencia y tecnología 2005-2006: Manual para el juzgamiento de proyectos de investigación en las ferias de ciencia y tecnología. San José, Costa Rica : MICIT.

Marshall, Ray and Tucker, Marc (1992). Thinking for a Living. Education and the Wealth of Nations. Nueva York: Basic Books.

Martin Serrano, Manuel (1978). Métodos de Investigación Social. Madrid: Akal Editor.

Mayor Sánchez, Antonio (1983). Bases para una Metodología Didáctica.2da Edición. San José: EUNED.

Mejía, Edilberto (1994). "Educación para el Nuevo Milenio ·. Costa Rica: Colegio Santa Fe.

Mejía, Marco Raul (1993). "Hacia un nuevo modelo educativo". In, Revista Universidad de Antioquía Vol. LXVII No.232. Medellín, pp 11-27

Motta Di Mare, Cecilia (1987). Seminario: Estrategias para hacer de la Administración un Motor Cambio en la Educación. Costa Rica, Ciudad Universitaria Rodrigo Facio.

Paniagua, Carlos German (1979). Principales Escuelas del Pensamiento Administrativo. San José: Editorial Universitaria Estatal a Distancia.

Paniagua, Carlos German (1980). "La Formación de Administradores para el Sistema Educativo Costarricense." San José C.R: U.C.R.

Pardinas, Felipe (1974). Metodología y Técnicas de Investigación en las Ciencias Sociales. 12th. Ed. México: Editorial Siglo XXI.

Piaget, J., L. Apostel et al (1986). Construcción y validación de las teorías científicas. Buenos Aires: Paidós.

Reich, Robert B (1993). El trabajo de las naciones. Hacia el capitalismo del Siglo XXI. Buenos Aires: Vergara.

Sagastume Gemmell, Marco Antonio (¿). El Arte de Hablar en Público. Guatemala: Talleres de Amisrael.

Sakaiya, Taichi (1994). Historia del Futuro. La sociedad del conocimiento. Santiago de Chile: Editorial Andrés Bello.

Sánchez Mora, Zaida (1984). "Análisis Temático de Editoriales de los Periódicos La Nación, La Prensa Libre, La República, del periódo 1978". San José: CEMIE-REDUC.

Silberman, M. (1998). Aprendizaje Activo. Adriana Oklander, translator. Buenos Aires: Editorial Troquel.

Smuts, Jan C (1926). Holism and Evolution, MacMillan, Compass.

Suárez, Patricia (2005). La Escritura Literaria 3rd Ed. Argentina: Homo Sapiens Ediciones.

Sylverman, Jay, Elaine Hughes and Diana Roberts Wienboer. Rules of Thumb. 2da. Ed. Estado Unidos: McGraw-Hill, 1993.

Tedesco, Juan Carlos (1993). "Tendances Actuelles des réformes educatives" In, Tierno Jiménez, Bernabé. Del Fracaso al Éxito Escolar. Barcelona: Plaza y Janés Editores.

Toffler, Alvin and Heidi (1995). Creating a New Civilization. Atlanta: Turner Publishing Inc.

UNESCO (1993). Informe Mundial sobre Educación. Madrid: Orymu, S.A.

UNESCO/OREALC (1993). "Hacia una nueva etapa de desarrollo educativo" En, Boletín 31. Proyecto Principal de Educación para América Latina y el Caribe (PROMEDLAC V). Santiago: Jun. 8-12.

Vasconcellos, María (1988). Le Système Educatif. París, Edition La Decouvert, pp. 3-13.